Winning Against Relapse

A Workbook of Action Plans for Recurring Health and Emotional Problems

Mary Ellen Copeland, PhD

Peach Press

Publishers Note

This publication is designed to provide accurate and authoritative information in regard to the subject matter covered. It is sold with the understanding that the publisher is not engaged in rendering psychological, financial, legal, or other professional services. If expert assistance or counseling is needed, the services of a competent professional should be sought.

Copyright © 1999 by Mary Ellen Copeland, PhD
Peach Press
P.O. Box 301
West Dummerston, VT 05357-0301

Cover Design © 2001 by Patti Smith.
Edited by Angela Watrous.
Text Design by Tracy Marie Powell
Library of Congress Catalog Card Number: 98-68745
ISBN: 0-9631366-5-8

Printed in the United States of America

Peach Press Website address: www.mentalhealthrecovery.com

This book is dedicated to Jane Winterling and Alan McNabb, who provided inspiration and ideas for it; and to numerous contributors, reviewers, editors, and all the dedicated people who attended the eight-day Recovery Series in Bradford, Vermont for their persistence in developing a monitoring and response system that really works.

Contents

Introduction

For the past nine years, I've been working with people who experience mild to severe psychiatric symptoms, often exacerbated by a wide variety of physical ailments, as well as with people who experience chronic pain.

This work is a result of my ongoing personal search for wellness and improvement in the quality of my life in spite of being diagnosed with manic depression, major depression, fibromyalgia, and chronic myofascial pain syndrome.

Twelve years ago, many years of high achievement and life enjoyment turned into confusion, frustration, and pain. I was unhappy with this unanticipated turn of events. I wanted my life back, to work and to play, to enjoy my family and friends.

My attempts to find out how people with these kinds of disorders cope on a day-to-day basis only served to increase my frustration. My psychiatrist first promised me this information, then told me that none existed. My medical doctor tried to convince me that the severe pain and other mysterious symptoms that were physically disabling me were "all in my head."

My persistence in searching for answers and compiling my findings for my use and for use by others has led me on a rewarding journey that has confirmed and affirmed my belief in the richness of the human experience. From publishing houses to major medical centers, from the backwoods of Alaska to the back wards of psychiatric hospitals, I've had the privileged of being invited into the lives of people whose courage and persistence continue to impress and inspire me.

Through this process of networking recovery information, I have uncovered ideas and strategies that, while safe and simple, have the capacity to create major life changes. As I continue to search for these strategies and share them with others, I am also in the process of teaching others to be mental health educators.

I was teaching recovery skills and strategies to a group of thirty patients, family members, and health care professionals as part of an eight-day educational program sponsored by the State Department of Mental Health in Vermont. They complained that the wellness process—that is, the process of developing and maintaining a lifestyle that helps prevent or minimize relapse—was too confusing. They felt it would be difficult to use the needed skills and strategies in their lives on a regular basis.

I spent several days working with this group, exploring possible systems that would facilitate the consistent use of these wellness skills and strategies. Together, we came up with a lot of ideas. The system described in this book, the Wellness Recovery Action Plan (WRAP), was the program that this group felt would be the most beneficial. Now thousands of people across the country are using this plan to deal with many different kinds of symptoms and issues.

WRAP has been so enthusiastically received that I decided to publish and distribute it so that it would be widely available. This plan is intended for use by anyone with chronic mental or physical health concerns. I use it consistently myself. It works very well for me.

Joan, a woman who lives with depression and is using the WRAP program, writes:

> I have a serious problem with depression. I've noticed when I start getting depressed I have certain kinds of thought patterns. These are not based on reality or are exaggerated responses to real events. These thought patterns have a profound effect on my depression and self-esteem. If I act as if they are true, I will "spiral down" until I cannot get out of my chair or feed myself. My thought patterns at this time are constantly of suicide. When I first started paying attention to my thought patterns, I noticed they would start with thoughts like, "I'm worthless and my life is worthless. I have no friends. No one loves me." The thoughts would come more often and more intensely and, as they did, I would become more self-loathing and hateful until I was in a crisis.
>
> Once I became aware of these thought patterns, I began to develop a WRAP. In my plan, I wrote down the negative things I say to myself and things I can say or do to counteract them, with the purpose of reaching out to counteract and change these negative thought patterns. I went to a few family members and friends. I explained how my depression worked and that I wanted them on my list of supporters. We have worked out an agreement so I can call them and they will tell me I have value to them.
>
> I knew my plan worked when a close friend of mine became involved with a man and instead of spending any time with me, she was spending all of her time with him. This triggered all those depressive thought patterns, and if I hadn't written them down and made plans, I probably would have needed hospitalization for treatment of severe depression. Instead, I called the people on my support list and made plans to get together with other friends. I didn't isolate myself as I would have in the past. I felt sad, but not bad.

Like Joan, I have also developed a WRAP for myself. I've been using it for two years to deal with recurring bouts of depression and the chronic pain of fibromyalgia. Previous to the development of this plan, I thought that I was doing a really good job of managing my life while "putting up" with time when the depression and pain seemed overwhelming. Now, because of my WRAP, I have fewer episodes of depression and pain. I also notice when these episodes are starting and I can use my WRAP to "nip them in the bud," before they get out of control and are much more difficult to manage. I change my WRAP often, as I become aware of new wellness strategies and alternative treatments. My WRAP has allowed me to create a revisable wellness strategy that allows me to recognize rather than ignore my triggers and early warning signs and respond to them with my own combination of techniques that work for me.

As you develop your plan, use all the resources that are available to you—books, magazines, the internet, the media, and information from family members, friends, and health care specialists. Your WRAP will belong to you. Use all of your creativity to make it into a plan that is tailored to meet your needs and enhance your wellness. You deserve to be well and happy.

Chapter 1

Understanding the Wellness Recovery Action Plan (WRAP)

What Is WRAP?

The Wellness Recovery Action Plan is a structured system for monitoring uncomfortable or distressing symptoms, as well as unhealthy habits or behavior patterns. Through planned responses, WRAP is also helpful in reducing, modifying, or eliminating those symptoms and/or creating the life change you want. It also includes instructions on developing advanced directives that instruct others on how to make decisions for you and to take care of and support you when your symptoms have made it impossible for you to do this for yourself.

Anecdotal reporting from people who are using this system indicates that by taking ongoing preventive action, responding to symptoms when they first appear rather than when they have become severe, and responding in ways that help to reduce, relieve, or eliminate the symptoms, their level of wellness and overall quality of life have improved significantly. In those cases where an illness can cause severe disability or be life threatening, those who have implemented WRAP into their lives report feeling that they are delaying the onset of more severe disability.

WRAP was initially developed for people with a variety of chronic psychiatric symptoms who were working hard to feel better and get on with their lives. I have shared the program with people with other illnesses and they agreed that it can be easily adapted for use with virtually any chronic mental or physical illness.

Jane Winterling has worked as a case worker in mental health programs for over twenty years and developed the initial concept for the Wellness Recovery Action Plan. She felt it was a plan that would help the people she works with—many of whom experience chronic psychiatric symptoms—get well, stay well, and improve the quality of their lives. When I told her I was writing this book, she agreed to help by lending some of her own thoughts and experiences. Jane describes WRAP as follows:

> WRAP is a structured way to learn about and plan for the process and/or stages of a problem or illness. Everything has a beginning, a middle, and an end. For example, when I was a young girl and my period started, it often took me by surprise. This led to some embarrassing moments. With time, experience, and knowledge, I began to recognize certain changes in my body and moods that let me know I needed to make sure I had some things in place. Many men have also experienced a time in adolescence when erections came at the drop of a hat. This led to some very embarrassing moments for them. With time, experience, and knowledge, they also came to learn to recognize early thoughts or feelings in their body that let them know it was time to think about or do something else.
>
> I use these examples because they are pretty universal and most everyone learns to deal with them successfully. In this same way, the recognition of subtle changes (which is a key component to WRAP), as well as talking to others for support and knowledge in order to reduce the anxiety and fear, are some of the same skills we need to deal with other, bigger problems.

WRAP will help you think about the stages/process of your problem or illness. It will help you to recognize those subtle changes or signs that signal the beginning of a relapse. For example, I learned my depression must be paid attention to when I start feeling emotionally disconnected from things that are important to me. This book also offers suggestions for tools you can use when these problems or symptoms arise, which you may wish to use in addition to any tools you have already discovered as you have dealt with issues in your life. With time and practice, you will find that you spend more time in the early stages of WRAP (i.e., following your daily maintenance plan, recognizing and responding to triggers, and recognizing and responding to early warning signs) and less in the acute stages (i.e., when things are breaking down and when in crisis).

One of the main components of WRAP is developing a daily maintenance plan, which includes things you must do daily in order to help prevent relapse. Jane Winterling talks about how she uses her daily maintenance plan to help prevent depression and burn out:

> I have worked in the mental health field for twenty years. I learned very soon and in a very painful way that I was susceptible to burnout. I realized that if I didn't develop a way to cope with this, I was going to have to change careers. Over the years, I have realized that there are some things that I must do on a regular, daily basis. If I do not do

these things, I am in trouble in about a month. If I do not pay attention, then I am looking at a serious depression that is going to last awhile, even if I go back to doing what I need to do, because I know it takes months to recover. Needless to say, I pay attention early. WRAP is designed to help you monitor uncomfortable, distressing symptoms and set up a lifestyle that assists you in avoiding relapse.

As you work on your WRAP, you will be developing various kinds of lists. There are forms provided in the book for you to write these lists on. You will find that there are duplicates of some of these forms in the appendix in the back of the book. You can complete the lists in the chapters themselves. Then, so you can have all of the forms together in one place, you may choose to photocopy the forms in the appendix and copy your responses onto the corresponding forms. Be sure you don't write directly in the appendix without first making a photocopy, as you will likely need to update your forms as time goes by, and this way you can simply make another copy of the blank forms. Or you can write your lists directly on these forms. You can also write your lists on lined three-ring binder paper. Choose whichever is easiest for you. You may find that you want to revise your plan from time to time. You can make new photocopies of the blank forms in the appendix to use for these revisions.

Before we continue, I'll give you a brief overview of the WRAP process. In chapter 2, you will create your own daily maintenance plan. This includes a description of how you feel when you feel well, a list of the things you need to do every day to maintain your wellness, and a list of things you might need to consider on a particular day. In addition, you can include lists of things you need to do several times a week, weekly, every other week, or monthly. This plan, which is meant to be used daily, will have components that remain the same every day and components that will need to be updated or changed each day.

In chapter 3, you will learn how to identify and act on triggers and early warning signs.

This chapter helps you identify those events or situations which, if they occur, might cause uncomfortable symptoms to begin. You will be asked to come up with a list of places, situations, or circumstances that could be avoided to limit exposure to triggers, as well as develop a plan of what to do if any of these triggers occur. The chapter will also teach you how to identify subtle early warning signs that may indicate the situation is beginning to worsen, and you will develop a plan of action to be used when any of these early warning signs are noticed. Finally, I will discuss how to deal with symptoms that occur when the situation has gotten much worse but has not yet reached a crisis—when you can still take action in your own behalf.

In chapter 4, you will develop a crisis plan. While WRAP is intended to reduce and minimize the symptoms of your ailment, it cannot always prevent relapse. By having a crisis plan, you are ensuring that you are cared for in the way you wish to be, and this will likely assist in a speedier recovery. Chapter 4 is multifaceted. It identifies those symptoms that indicate you can no longer continue to make decisions, take care of yourself, and keep yourself safe. It is for use by supporters and health care professionals on your behalf.

In developing your individualized crisis plan, first you will provide information that defines what you are like when you are well. Then you will identify those symptoms that indicate others need to take over responsibility for your care, name those supporters, and specify their roles. Next, you will indicate those medications which, if necessary, are all right with you, those which are not, and the reasons why. You will have the opportunity to record your preferences regarding the options of developing a home care, community care, or other type of care plan to use in lieu of hospitalization. You will also be asked to list the treatments and treatment facilities which, if necessary, are all right with you, those which are not, and the reasons why. You will be given the opportunity to develop an intensive description of what is wanted—and what is not wanted—from supporters when symptoms become this intense. Finally, you will provide information for supporters to use in determining when you no longer need to use your crisis plan.

Chapters 5 through 8 will lead you through the steps necessary to create a nurturing lifestyle that helps minimize relapse. Chapter 5 will introduce you to tools and strategies that are helpful in reducing symptoms and dealing with counterproductive thoughts and feelings. Chapter 6 will lead you through the steps necessary in creating a support system of family, friends, and health care providers. Chapter 7 helps you increase your positive feelings about yourself and combat those which are negative; self-esteem and well-being are directly linked to issues of mental and physical health. Chapter 8 provides exercises which can be used on a daily basis for stress and tension reduction.

Chapter 9 will assist you in adapting WRAP for any special needs and circumstances you may have. For example, reading or writing problems, disabilities, homelessness, sudden change in circumstances, or coping with a severe loss. Chapter 10, a chapter for health care providers, focuses on helping individuals and/or groups of people develop personal action plans.

The appendix includes blank copies of all of the exercises you may need to refer to after completing the book. Finally, at the end of the book you will find a Resources section that will give you additional information on developing tools and strategies for your action plans. All of my previous books are listed here, and you may especially wish to refer to them if you have problems with depression, worry, or fibromyalgia and chronic myofascial pain syndrome.

Who Can Benefit from Using WRAP?

WRAP can be used by anyone who wants to deal with and recover from any illness, condition, or set of circumstances that are interfering with the quality of their life. It can also be used to keep yourself well on an ongoing basis, preventing the onset of chronic or acute illness, general poor health, or ineffective and troublesome behavior patterns.

The illnesses, disorders, or lifestyle difficulties that WRAP can help address or guide your recovery from include, but are not limited to, the following (check those that apply to you):

❏ chronic overwork   ❏ completing an advanced degree

❏ unemployment   ❏ adjustment to retirement

❏ adjustment to a chronic illness ❏ social isolation

- ❏ juggling too many responsibilities
- ❏ addictions
- ❏ diabetes
- ❏ Cushing's syndrome
- ❏ lupus
- ❏ chronic myofascial pain syndrome (MPS)
- ❏ multiple sclerosis
- ❏ post-concussion syndrome
- ❏ seizures
- ❏ mononucleosis
- ❏ chronic fatigue syndrome (CFS)
- ❏ seasonal affective disorder (SAD)
- ❏ irritable bowel syndrome
- ❏ candida infection
- ❏ hepatitis
- ❏ stroke
- ❏ all kinds of cancer
- ❏ manic depression
- ❏ surgery
- ❏ ongoing medical treatments
- ❏ tuberculosis
- ❏ giardiasis
- ❏ chronic poisoning
- ❏ drug interactions

- ❏ living "two lives"
- ❏ endocrine disorders
- ❏ Addison's disease
- ❏ rheumatoid or osteoarthritis
- ❏ fibromyalgia (FMS)
- ❏ acquired immunodeficiency syndrome (AIDS)
- ❏ recovery from an accident
- ❏ post-polio syndrome
- ❏ viral infections
- ❏ malaria
- ❏ Parkinson's disease
- ❏ gastrointestinal disorders
- ❏ incontinence
- ❏ kidney diseases
- ❏ heart disease
- ❏ macular degeneration
- ❏ depression
- ❏ schizophrenia
- ❏ chemotherapy
- ❏ chronic pain
- ❏ dysentery
- ❏ chemical sensitivity
- ❏ drug side effects
- ❏ vitamin and mineral deficiencies

- ❏ other illnesses or disorders you have that you plan to combat with WRAP:

_____

_____

_____

_____

This plan can also be used to address addictions, which include, but are not limited to, the following (check those that apply to you):

❏ alcohol   ❏ drugs

❏ food   ❏ gambling

❏ prescription or nonprescription
   medications

❏ other addictions you have that you plan to combat with WRAP:

_____

_____

_____

_____

WRAP can be used to work on a variety of health issues, including, but not limited to, the following:

❏ losing or gaining weight   ❏ improving diet

❏ developing an exercise program   ❏ increasing stamina

❏ reducing fatigue   ❏ getting more high quality sleep

❏ other health issues you have that you plan to combat with WRAP:

_____

_____

_____

_____

WRAP can also serve as your day-to-day guide for working on personal and growth-oriented issues such as (check those that apply to you):

❏ raising self-esteem and   ❏ changing negative thoughts to
   self-confidence   positive ones

❏ developing a strong support   ❏ learning to advocate effectively
   system   for yourself

❏ making new friends   ❏ learning to be more assertive

❏ enhancing your relationships with   ❏ letting go of workaholic
   family members and friends   tendencies

❏ improving the overall quality of   ❏ increasing vocational
   your life   competencies

❏ moving ahead   ❏ enriching your life

❏ other personal or growth-oriented issues you have that you plan to address with WRAP:

_____

_____

_____

_____

It is important to remember that WRAP is not a replacement for good professional care, though it *is* a safe and wise addition to any chosen course of treatment. Following is a list of many of the applications of WRAP (check off those that apply to you). Answer the following question—I would like to use WRAP to:

❏ keep myself well on an ongoing basis.

❏ recover from an illness or surgery such as mononucleosis, hepatitis, meningitis, open heart surgery, appendicitis, etc. Describe your particular concerns here:

_____

_____

_____

❏ prevent or delay the return of physical or emotional symptoms that you have experienced in the past, such as depression, diabetes, and pain. Describe your particular concerns here:

_____

_____

_____

❏ prevent deterioration or health decline that accompanies some illnesses or conditions, such as arthritis, multiple sclerosis, macular degeneration, or lupus. Describe your particular concerns here:

_____

_____

_____

❑ prolong remission or periods of time when symptoms are absent, as experienced in ailments such as cancer and fibromyalgia and myofascial pain syndrome. Describe your particular concerns here:

_____

_____

_____

❑ decrease the intensity of physical or psychological pain. Describe your particular concerns here:

_____

_____

_____

❑ create positive change in the way you feel, such as healing from a loss, undergoing a physical or emotional trauma, or trying to improve your self-esteem. Describe your particular concerns here:

_____

_____

_____

❑ increase your overall wellness by beginning an exercise program or trying to lose weight. Describe your particular concerns here:

_____

_____

_____

❑ increase your enjoyment of life by breaking old patterns like workaholism or isolation. Describe your particular concerns here:

_____

_____

_____

❑ let go of addictive behaviors like alcoholism, smoking, gambling, or drug use. Describe your particular concerns here:

_____

_____

_____

One commonly overlooked ailment is burnout, which is caused by working too hard or under too much stress without taking time to take care of yourself.

Burnout, if not addressed, will interfere with day-to-day functioning and might even cause a more serious illness. Using the example of burnout, I'd like to demonstrate how WRAP can be used to help minimize a particular problem.

The symptoms of burn out often mimic a physical or psychological disorder. They include (check any that apply to you):

❏ irritability

❏ increased anxiety

❏ feeling "spaced out"

❏ feeling helpless, hopeless, and worthless

❏ decreased ability to make decisions

❏ anger

❏ nothing seems worthwhile

❏ disturbed sleep

❏ poor memory

❏ racing thoughts

❏ feeling emotionally disconnected to things that have meaning in your life

❏ feeling like a failure at everything

❏ edginess

❏ feeling overwhelmed

Let's say, for example, that as you think about your symptoms, you realize you are becoming or are already burned out. Then you would develop your individualized WRAP program to address burnout, as well as any other issues you wish to focus on directly.

Unfortunately, many people respond to burnout by trying harder at everything, a strategy that is bound to fail. Your plans of what you need to do for yourself every day might include eating healthy foods, avoiding junk food, getting enough rest and sleep, getting some exercise and doing something you enjoy. If the symptoms increase, or are triggered by some unexpected event, you could use WRAP to develop ways of responding to these increased symptoms or this event that will keep your feelings of burnout from increasing. If, in spite of your efforts, the symptoms do increase, you would have more intense plans of things that you can do that will keep your situation from becoming a crisis, the kind of crisis that might prevent you from working or result in you losing your job or developing a stress-related illness or injury. Then you would develop a plan for your family members and friends to use if the situation should deteriorate to the point where you could no longer make good decisions for yourself or take care of yourself (this used to be called a nervous breakdown).

If you followed your plan, you would likely notice that the feelings that indicated that you were burned out would begin to abate. If the strategies didn't work, you would have a crisis plan that could be put into place if needed. Then, when you were feeling somewhat better, you would need to go back to the drawing board and develop a plan that will work for you in the future.

Try to be realistic about how much time this process will take. Jane Winterling says:

When I was in my twenties, I lived near an elderly New Hampshire farmer. As I would tell him all the things I needed to do, wanted to do, etc., he would look at me and say, "And when did you want that done? Yesterday!" Those words have helped me innumerable times in my life when I get going too fast and nothing seems to be "keeping up."

Use the following form to make a condensed list of the issues you want to address using WRAP (include all of the items you've checked off or listed in this chapter that you want to include in your WRAP). There is a blank copy of this form in the appendix, so you can modify your goals as your needs change.

I want to use my WRAP to address the following issues:

_____

_____

_____

_____

Preparing to Develop Your Individualized WRAP

As you begin developing your WRAP, try to look at your level of wellness as part of a continuum—from feeling quite well without serious issues of physical and emotional health, to a place where these issues have become so difficult that they are interfering with every aspect of my life. By using this more complete picture as a basis for analyzing hard times, you will likely be able to take steps to intercede earlier and return to your optimal level of wellness more quickly.

As you go through the following chapters, you will need a few additional materials to optimally use WRAP:

1. An inexpensive three-ring binder, one inch thick. I prefer the kind that has a pocket for inserting papers in the inside of the front and back covers. You can use these pockets for copies of medical records, information about medications, generic daily maintenance plans, etc. You will use this binder to keep the primary forms from your WRAP in one, easily accessible place (these forms are the ones duplicated in the appendix).

2. A set of five dividers or tabs.

3. A package of three-ring filler paper (most people preferred lined paper). If you prefer to use your computer, you can buy three-ring paper for your printer or punch the paper yourself.

4. A pen or pencil.

5. Friends, family members, or other supporters to give you ideas and support.

Once you have these materials, you will be ready to move on to chapter 2, Creating Your Daily Maintenance Plan.

Chapter 2

Creating Your Daily Maintenance Plan

How Can a Daily Maintenance Plan Help?

You may have already discovered that there are certain things you need to do *every day* to maintain your wellness. Writing them down and reminding yourself to do these things on a daily basis is an important step toward wellness. A daily maintenance plan helps you recognize those things that you need to do to remain healthy and plan your days accordingly. Also, when things have been going well for a while and you notice you are starting to feel worse, it's extremely helpful to have a written reference to remind you of what you can do to get better. This way, when you are starting to feel out of sorts, you may be able to trace it back to not doing something on your daily maintenance plan.

A daily maintenance plan can help you set priorities. Jane Winterling shares how she recognized the devastating effect that burnout has had on her life:

> Knowing what I had to do to keep from getting burned out made it easier to tell myself not to do things that increase my chances of becoming burned out. I learned that I didn't have the energy to do all the things I thought I could do. It also helps to organize the chaotic mess I end up with when trying to lead a "normal" life and manage recurring depression.

A daily maintenance plan may seem unnecessary or bothersome, and you may be tempted to skip or skim over it. However, for me and many others, it provides a daily structure that ensures we are taking optimal care of ourselves. In addition, it may also help you more easily address and deal with the changes in your life brought on by long-term illness, even when the illness is in remission. A daily maintenance plan is an acknowledgment of those changes. Often the hardest part of a chronic illness is the acceptance of the limits you now face, but the good news is that once you accept these new circumstances, you can use WRAP to readjust and increase your overall well-being.

Setting Up Your Own Daily Maintenance Plan

How Would You Like to Feel?

Take out your three-ring binder and dividers. On the first divider tab write "daily maintenance plan." Insert it in the binder along with several sheets of filler paper. On the first sheet of paper write a description of how you feel when you are well or how you feel on a good day.

If you have been sick or unhealthy for some time, you may have forgotten what it feels like when you are well. For many years I experienced severe mood swings. Even when I wasn't experiencing acute symptoms, I felt tired and out of sorts. I couldn't even remember what it was like to feel well.

If you are having this problem, write down what you would like to feel like or be like if you were well. You'll be able to use your daily maintenance plan and other parts of WRAP to become the way you'd like to be. For example, if you would like to be more friendly, your daily maintenance list might include smiling twice each day at people you don't know and being in touch with a friend at least once a day.

While writing your description about how you feel when you are well and/or how you'd like to feel, try to use a list format to make it simple and straightforward. A simple list of adjectives works very well. This list will remind you during the hard times of what it is you are working toward. You may want to start your list with the words: "When I feel well, I am ..."

The following descriptive words are examples of words that you may want to use on your list. Check those that apply to you and write them on page one of your binder along with any others you have thought of:

❏ happy

❏ cheerful

❏ outgoing

❏ active

❏ humorous

❏ enjoy discussion

❏ playful

❏ bright

❏ talkative

❏ boisterous

❏ energetic

❏ a jokester

❏ flirtatious

❏ enjoy crowds

❏ dramatic

❏ adventurous

❏ optimistic

❏ responsible

❏ capable

❏ curious

❏ analytical

❏ ambitious

❏ careful

❏ friendly

❏ easy to get along with

❏ accepting of life

❏ willing to risk

❏ quick thinking

❏ a fast learner

❏ thoughtful

❏ reflective

❏ fluid

❏ contemplative

❏ calm

❏ hopeful

❏ introverted

❏ breathe easily

❏ flamboyant

❏ physically active

❏ reasonable

❏ competent

❏ industrious

❏ interested

❏ enjoy learning

❏ perceptive

❏ handy

❏ supportive to others

❏ tolerant

❏ able to work

❏ quick acting

❏ flexible

❏ warm-hearted

❏ imaginative

❏ resourceful

❏ creative

❏ peaceful

❏ comfortable alone

❏ quiet

❏ reserved

Now make a list, including those you have checked and any other attributes you have when you feel well. Put a copy of the following form in your binder (there is a blank copy available in the appendix):

When I feel well, I am:

_____

_____

_____

_____

Whenever you are feeling discouraged, refer back to this list. Read it over several times. Try to remember that you are a special person and you deserve the very best out of life. You may choose to share this list with friends, family members, and health care professionals who have a hard time remembering what you were like when you were well.

Your Daily Maintenance List

There are certain things, such as getting enough sleep and doing something you enjoy, that can increase your level of wellness significantly when done on a daily basis. Making a commitment to yourself to do these kinds of things daily will help keep you healthy and allow you to do the things you want to do. Writing out a list of these things and reviewing it every day can keep you on target.

Many people who use WRAP regularly report that the daily maintenance list is the most important part of the plan. By following it faithfully, they have successfully addressed the issues that needed attention and/or noticed a significant reduction in the severity and/or rate of occurrence of the symptoms.

If your family's lifestyle when you were a child was hectic, chaotic, and disorganized, you may not have had an opportunity to learn many of the skills you need as an adult to accomplish your goals and make your life the way you want it to be. A daily maintenance plan can provide the structure, organization, and discipline you need to make your life more organized.

Taking the time to do the things on your daily maintenance list is so much better than wasting time being sick, being in pain, or just not feeling "up to snuff." Developing a daily maintenance plan is also a way to set and develop priorities. It can prevent you from becoming overwhelmed by trying to do too much, while still taking care of the things you need to do each day to stay well. In assessing what you can get done in a day, it helps to first list each activity you currently do daily, and estimate how much time it requires.

To assure that you are developing a reasonable plan—one that you will actually be able to implement—make a list in the following exercise of all the activities you do every day and how much time they take, including those you already know you want on your daily maintenance list. If you find that you don't have time to do all these activities—the sum total is over twenty-four hours—you may have to revise your daily schedule or your daily maintenance plan. You may find that in order to take good care of yourself or create the changes you want in your life, you may have to spend less time involved in activities like working, watching television, or housecleaning. Or you may need to be flexible with activities such as exercise, fitting them in at different times.

My old schedule might have looked like this: six hours for sleeping, fourteen hours for work, two hours for housekeeping and fixing meals, one hour for meals, and one hour to take care of myself—not nearly enough time to exercise, do something fun, get in touch with a friend, get some outside light, and do a meditation exercise. My new daily maintenance plan, developed and revised over time, includes: eight hours for sleeping, eight hours for work, one hour to spend with friends and family members, one hour for a fun activity, one hour for exercise and outdoor light, one hour for a relaxation exercise and journaling, two hours for housekeeping and meal preparation, and two hours for meals—a much more reasonable and healthy lifestyle.

You may have different days when your schedules aren't the same (i.e. working days and weekends, days off or holidays). You may find that it is helpful to have different daily maintenance plans for these different kinds of days. For instance, on the days when you are at work, your daily maintenance may have to be more limited or contain some activities and reminders that you don't need on days when you are not working. You may have time for only thirty minutes of exercise during your lunch break, thirty minutes later in the day to do something fun, and time for a brief check-in with a supporter. You may want to add to your daily maintenance plan the task of getting your clothes ready for the next day, as well as a reminder to limit your work to eight hours or less a day. On the days that you are not working, you may want to schedule in more time for exercise, fun activities, and getting together with supporters. If this is the case, you can develop two plans—one for the days you are working and one for the days you are not.

Your Daily Routine
(Integrating Current and Desired Activities)

Activity	Time (hours or minutes)

Now make a list of things you know you need to do for yourself every day to keep yourself feeling as well as possible. They are different for each person, but this list of options may help you decide what you want to include on your daily maintenance list. The amounts and times listed are only examples; change them to best meet your specific needs. Check those items that apply to you:

❏   eat three healthy meals and three healthy snacks

❏   eat six servings of whole grain foods

❑ eat five servings of vegetables

❑ eat two or three servings of fruit

❑ eat smaller portions of protein at each meal

❑ drink at least six eight-ounce glasses of water

❑ avoid caffeine, sugar, junk foods, and/or alcohol

❑ exercise for at least thirty minutes

❑ get exposure to outdoor light for at least thirty minutes

❑ take medications

❑ take nutritional supplements: vitamins, minerals, amino acids, herbs, etc.

❑ have twenty minutes of relaxation or meditation time

❑ write in a journal for fifteen minutes

❑ spend at least thirty minutes enjoying a fun, affirming, and/or creative activity

❑ get support from someone you can be real with

❑ check in with your partner for at least twenty minutes

❑ check in with your housemate(s) for at least ten minutes

❑ check in with yourself for at least twenty minutes (how are you doing physically, emotionally, and/or spiritually?)

❑ ask yourself what you need to do that day

❑ go to work

❑ do something nice for someone else

❑ clean up after yourself

❑ record a dream from the previous night

❑ do stretching and breathing exercises

❑ spend time alone doing nothing

In the following form, write in these and/or any of your own activities that you feel you must do daily to achieve optimum wellness. There is a duplicate copy of this form in the appendix.

Your daily maintenance plan (things you must do every day):

_____

_____

_____

_____

_____

_____

_____

_____

Your Daily Reminder List

Now make a reminder list for things you might need to do. These are not things you need to do every day, but sometimes they may be very important to your overall wellness and sense of well-being. Reviewing this list daily can reduce the stress caused by forgetting tasks that need to be done or that would make you feel better if you did them.

One man reported that he often forgot to pay his bills on time. The pink slips and phone calls caused him a great deal of stress. Paying bills wasn't something he needed to do every day, but on some days it was very important. By reviewing his list of things he might need to do, he was reminded and began paying his bills in a timely manner.

A person with a chronic illness reported that she often forget to order a prescription, which means that one or several doses of a medication that needs to be taken consistently are missed. This often exacerbates symptoms and is generally hard on the body. This list serves as a reminder to prevent this situation.

Many people who live alone reported that they have a hard time with loneliness on the weekend when others are involved in family-oriented activities. During the week they are busily occupied at work and loneliness is not an issue. Through the reminder list, they remember early in the week that it would be helpful to make some plans in advance for the weekend. Then they have ample time to arrange outings with friends and family members like movies, concerts, picnics, and hikes and planning interesting projects and excursions for the time when they are alone.

The following suggestions will give you ideas to put on your list along with others you wish to add.

"Today, do I need to (or would it be good to)":

❏ get a massage

❏ set up an appointment with one of my health care professionals

❏ write some letters

❏ spend time with children

❏ do peer counseling

❏ call my sponsor

❏ plan something fun for the weekend

❏ be in touch with my family

❏ spend time with animals

❏ get more sleep

❏ do some housework

❏ do the laundry

❏ take a hot bubble bath

❏ plan something fun for the evening

❏ spend some time with my counselor, case manager, sponsor, etc.

❏ go to a twelve-step meeting or support group

❏ plan a vacation

❏ health-related testing

❏ checking in with a physician or health care professional

❏ working out at the gym

❏ buy groceries

❏ have some personal time

❏ spend time with a good friend

❏ spend more time with my partner

❏ go out for a long walk or do some other extended outdoor activity (gardening, biking, swimming, fishing, etc.)

❏ remember someone's birthday or anniversary

❏ shopping for groceries

❏ medication check-ins

❏ quality time with my partner or children

Your Daily Optional Reminder List (a duplicate copy of this form is available in the appendix):

"Today I *might* need to":

_____

_____

_____

_____

_____

For things you need to do several times a week it may help to do them on the same days every week. For instance if you need to water your houseplants twice a week you might do it on Sunday and Thursday.

Now create optional reminder lists of things you need to do weekly, every other week, or monthly. Failure to keep appointments and to do the things you need to do to take care of yourself can create added stress in your life, causing or worsening symptoms and decreasing the quality of your life. Regular review and attention to these activities is a positive step toward increasing wellness and improving the quality of your life.

Weekly activities might include:

❏ paying bills   ❏ physical therapy

❏ counseling   ❏ acupressure

❏ acupuncture   ❏ art therapy

❏ dance therapy   ❏ support group meetings

❏ phone calls to family members or   ❏ visits to elderly or ill family
   friends   members and friends

❏ house cleaning

Your Weekly Reminder List (a duplicate copy of this form is available in the appendix):

Activity	Day of the week

Activities that need to take place every other week might include:

❏ doctors appointments   ❏ counseling appointments

❏ paying bills   ❏ fill the car with gas

❏ mowing the lawn   ❏ maintaining contact with
                                            supporters

Your Biweekly Reminder List (a duplicate copy of this form is available in the appendix):

Activity	When

Monthly activities might include:

❏ paying bills   ❏ health care appointments

❏ car maintenance   ❏ home maintenance

❏ hair care

Your Monthly Reminder List (a duplicate copy of this form is available in the appendix):

Activity	When

You have now completed the first section of your daily maintenance plan. For many people it is the "backbone" of their WRAP. They find that continuous use of this section keeps them from having to use other sections of the book. When it stops working for you, you can tear out the pages and write some new ones.

You will be surprised at how much better you will feel after taking just these few positive steps on your own behalf.

Chapter 3

Identifying Triggers, Early Warning Signs, and Signs of Potential Crisis

Triggers

Identifying Your Triggers

Each of us carries with us a personal history of life experiences—some good, some bad. When something happens in life that *triggers* memories of these life experiences, especially if they were traumatic experiences that were frightening or dangerous, you may lose track of what your life is currently like, and feel as if you are back at the time when the event was happening. You react to the present as if you were in the past. You may remember the event or events, or you may not remember the events.

Take the following story, for example. A businessman was audited by the Internal Revenue Service (IRS). This involved long, painful interviews in which he was grilled about every aspect of his financial life. He was given fines and penalties and subsequently fired his accountant. It took him some time to hire a new accountant, trying to do his books on his own in the meantime. The new accountant, not knowing his history, brings him a new form from the IRS which, if filled out, will save him considerable money. On hearing the letters IRS, the man goes into a rage, telling the accountant that if he is audited, he will sue him. The accountant leaves stunned and humiliated. The relationship with the accountant becomes strained as he cannot share any new information that might save the businessman money for fear of another outburst. In a year he tells the businessman he can no longer keep his books.

It is only in being aware of this history, or realizing that something has happened in your past that set off this reaction, that you can make plans and consciously separate the past from the present. This takes time. Often you are not aware that you are reacting to your history or being triggered until it has happened. In trying to cope with these triggers, some people abuse substances, misuse prescribed medications, have rages, isolate themselves from others, feel very nervous and anxious, or have panic attacks. The events that set off these chain reactions of behaviors, thoughts, and feelings are called "triggers."

Triggers are external events or circumstances that may produce symptoms or feelings that may be very uncomfortable or distressing, or that may worsen an already existing condition. Sometimes we feel as if they make us go "backwards" or throw us into a "downward spiral." These things happen to everyone. No one is completely immune to triggers. It is possible to protect yourself from some triggers, like avoiding an abusive person or staying out of a frightening neighborhood, but some of them are unavoidable, no matter how much you structure and take care with your life.

The feelings that come up may be normal reactions to different kinds of events in our lives, but they demand a countering response in order to maintain wellness. The awareness of this susceptibility and the development of plans to deal with triggering events when they come up will increase your ability to deal effectively with these triggers.

In this section of WRAP, you will identify your triggers and write them on your triggers list. Some helpful ways to do this include:

• reviewing the list of triggers provided and writing on your list any that you feel are triggers for you

• thinking back to difficult times you have had in the past and looking at external events that may have caused these difficult times (e.g., the death of a loved one may have "triggered" a serious increase in symptoms)

• asking family members and friends for ideas on external events they feel may have caused an increase in your symptoms (i.e., your friend might remember that your divorce or breakup preceded a deep depression)

• noticing those things on a daily basis that cause you to feel upset or stressed (i.e., getting a big bill in the mail or being treated rudely by a family member)

You may want to carry a small notebook with you through the day and jot down triggers as you think of them, as you are talking to people or dealing with your daily responsibilities, transferring them to the list in your binder when it is convenient. Listing your triggers helps you understand your personal triggers so that you notice them right away and respond quickly, with the intention of avoiding an increase in your symptoms. After you have identified your triggers and transferred them to your list, I will discuss how you can develop a plan for responding to these triggers so they will not cause an increase in your symptoms in the future.

On the next tab in your binder, write "Triggers." Your triggering events may be included in the following list. You may have noticed that these sorts of events have been unsettling for you in the past. If so, check them and then transfer them to your list, adding other triggers that you have recognized:

❑ anniversary dates of losses or trauma

❑ being overly tired

❑ work stress

❑ spending too much time alone

❑ being teased or put down

❑ physical illness like a cold or the flu

❑ loud noises

❑ angry outbursts by others

❑ being in an intimate situation

❑ someone trying to tell you how to run your life

❑ self-blame

❑ losing the use of a limb, organ, or sense

❑ continuing to work when overly tired

❑ upsetting world events

❑ family friction

❑ being judged or criticized

❑ financial problems

❑ being reminded of abandonment or deprivation

❑ being made a scapegoat

❑ being around abusive behavior

❑ excessive stress

❑ extreme guilt (for example, from saying "no.")

❑ not being validated

❑ fear of worsening of symptoms and resulting consequences such as invasive treatments, hospitalization, and detoxification

Using any of the suggested triggers that you feel apply to you and any others you have noticed in your life, fill in the following form:

Your List of Triggers (a copy of this form is provided in the appendix):

_____

_____

_____

_____

_____

One way of dealing with triggers is to reduce your exposure to them. For example, if Janet gets overly tired, she gets upset easily. She finds that she can't deal with small things that wouldn't usually bother her. She might respond to a family member in an irrational way. They get offended, she feels badly, she gives herself some negative self-talk, and the situation worsens. In this instance, her exhaustion triggers her irritation. To reduce her likelihood of being triggered in this manner, it's important for Janet to work on getting plenty of rest.

There are many ways people get triggered. Sam, for instance, finds that every time she visits her sister's family, they talk about incidences of incest that happened many years ago. It brings up bad memories for Sam and triggers her to feel irritated and angry. This leads her into a downward spiral of depression that she finds difficult to recover from. Talking about these incidents of incest are triggers for Sam. They cause an increase in disturbing flashbacks and nightmares.

Other kinds of triggers may be less psychological and more physiological. For example, Jim has asthma. Hot, muggy weather and certain kinds of weather inversions worsen his symptoms. He attempts to lessen his exposure to those triggers by spending little time outdoors when the weather conditions are unsuitable, living in the most appropriate climate possible, and having air conditioning in his home.

Avoiding Your Triggers

Once you have a working list of your triggers, you are ready to make a list of things you can do to avoid or limit your exposure to possible triggering events. They could include (check those that apply to you and make any specifications necessary):

❑ certain people

❑ certain kinds of work

❑ particular kinds of exercise

❑ getting overly tired

❑ certain kinds of events

❑ watching the news on television or listening to it on the radio

❑ bars

❑ construction sites (or other loud places)

❑ freeways

❑ smoggy places

❑ hot, dry places

❑ cold places

❑ forested areas

❑ places where the terrain isn't comfortable to you (e.g., very steep, rocky, flat, etc.)

❑ certain places

❑ violent movies

❑ particular kinds of activity

❑ extended travel

❑ reading the newspaper

❑ lifting more than a certain amount of weight

❑ big crowds

❑ malls and large stores, or certain kinds of stores

❑ small places

❑ cloudy, wet, rainy places

❑ hot, damp places

❑ snowy places

❑ dark, poorly lit places

❑ places where there is a lot of noise and confusion

Use the following to list what you wish to avoid to prevent being triggered. This list should include any of the previous examples that apply, as well as any others you can add.

Things to avoid to prevent being triggered:

_____

_____

_____

_____

_____

_____

Coping with Triggers When They Occur

Triggers are often something that you can't completely plan for or avoid. Because of this, it helps to develop a plan of what you can do if those triggers come up—a plan that can keep these triggers from worsening your overall health and sense of well-being.

Following is an example of how Maya coped with her trigger of getting a bill that was larger than she anticipated. She received a bill for some dental work. It was twenty dollars more than she expected and more than she could afford. Immediately, she had a clutching, anxious feeling in her chest. Rather than spend the afternoon fretting over the situation, she referred to her WRAP binder and found her ideas for coping with triggers. Choosing one, she sat down, took a few deep breaths, and did a focusing exercise. The deep breaths had an immediate calming effect and the focusing exercise helped her realize that she was feeling quite stressed out about money. Just knowing that gave her some relief. Then, through the questions that are part of the focusing exercise, she discovered action she could take—calling the dentist to ask about the discrepancy, and, if the bill was accurate, arranging a reasonable payment schedule.

The following list, which includes many wellness "tools" that will be described more in detail in later chapters, may provide you with some ideas for coping with triggers:

- ❏ talking to someone you trust about what's bothering you
- ❏ exercise
- ❏ light
- ❏ brainstorming
- ❏ get a physi examination

- ❏ educating yourself about your illness
- ❏ diet
- ❏ daily planning
- ❏ do something normal
- ❏ get a medication check

- ❏ talk to a health care professional about a change in your treatment regime
- ❏ get a referral to a specialist
- ❏ supportive therapies
- ❏ give yourself a massage
- ❏ acupressure
- ❏ get professional counseling
- ❏ call a hot line
- ❏ ask someone else to help you out
- ❏ have a meeting of your supporters or your family
- ❏ wear something that makes you feel good
- ❏ make a collage (or other artistic expression) of your life
- ❏ spend ten minutes writing down everything good you can think of about yourself
- ❏ do something special for someone else
- ❏ get some little things done
- ❏ yoga
- ❏ do relaxation and stress reduction exercises
- ❏ play with children or a pet
- ❏ take a warm bath
- ❏ deep breathing
- ❏ call a support person and ask them to listen while you talk through the situation
- ❏ exposing yourself to something that smells good to you
- ❏ listening to music

- ❏ vitamin, mineral, herbal, homeopathic, or other food supplementation
- ❏ hot or cold packs
- ❏ get a massage
- ❏ acupuncture
- ❏ getting a second opinion
- ❏ get peer counseling
- ❏ call a warm line
- ❏ host a potluck supper or some other meal
- ❏ do something that makes you laugh
- ❏ look through old pictures, scrapbooks, and photo albums
- ❏ make a list of your accomplishments
- ❏ surround yourself with people who are positive, affirming, and loving
- ❏ pretend you are your own best friend
- ❏ repeat positive affirmations
- ❏ being present in the moment
- ❏ look at something pretty or that means something special to you
- ❏ do focusing exercises
- ❏ do breathing awareness exercises
- ❏ progressive relaxation exercises
- ❏ auralizing (similar to visualization, but involves imagining sound instead of sight)
- ❏ do some deep breathing exercises
- ❏ play a musical instrument

❏ get some vigorous exercise (i.e., playing basketball or swimming)

❏ make sure you do everything on your daily maintenance program

❏ guided imagery

❏ visualization

❏ work on changing negative thoughts to positive ones

❏ get validation from someone you feel close to

❏ pray or meditate

❏ write in a journal

❏ go for a walk

❏ do a focusing exercise

❏ take an hour-long time-out in a comfortable place

❏ spend at least an hour involved in a creative activity

❏ go to a community activity

❏ sing and/or dance

Other ways to cope with your triggers:

_____

_____

_____

_____

_____

Using the responses from this list and others that you have discovered, develop a plan of things that you can do whenever you experience a trigger to keep you from feeling badly or worsening your symptoms. It may include some things you know you must do, like taking a few deep breaths, doing a focusing exercise, taking a walk, and talking to a supporter. It could also include some things you can do if you have time, like spending an hour playing the piano or working in your garden. After you have used the plan a few times, reevaluate how it's working. You may find that some of your responses are very helpful and some are not. You can change this plan to meet your needs.

By developing a plan like this, you intervene and take positive action at a time when it is easy to do, before the situation has escalated or worsened.

Your Plan for Responding to Triggers

_____

_____

_____

_____

Once you've completed this section, you may want to transfer your plan onto a photocopy of the exercises (copied from the appendix) and put it in your binder. Then, congratulate yourself! You have just completed another significant part of your WRAP. Take some time to do something really nice for yourself. Go to a good movie, spend some time with a friend, or work in your flower garden—whatever feels really good to you.

Early Warning Signs

Early warning signs are those subtle signs of change that indicate you may need to take action to avoid a worsening of your condition or situation. They are changes in the way you think, act, and/or feel. They may seem to come "out of the blue," unrelated to stressful events. The problem with early warning signs is that they are often ignored or go unnoticed. They may be so subtle you are not even aware of them, or you may not see them initially as connected with your condition.

Using WRAP, Caroline began making a concerted effort to stop her downward spiral of recurring episodes of deep depression by reviewing her day-to-day life prior to the worsening of her depression. By doing this, she became aware of a very significant warning sign—one which is very easy for her to identify and monitor. She realized that, for her, failure to look both ways before crossing the street is an early warning sign—a change in the way she acts. It came to her attention when she realized that sometimes people she was walking with would grab her coat or warn her of oncoming traffic as she was about to step off of the curb. This is not necessary when she is feeling fine—she always looks both ways before she crosses the street. Tuning into this allowed her to take action early, before her depression worsened and became more difficult to treat. Once she identifies this early warning sign, she can easily recognize it whenever it occurs. When it does, she refers to her WRAP and does those things that have helped her in the past, like getting together with good friends and working on a quilting project.

John, who has Parkinson's disease, was using WRAP to work on changing his negative thoughts to positive ones. He became aware that his negative thinking increased when he hadn't been able to sleep well, as well as when he feels slightly anxious all the time. After identifying this, he was able to enhance his wellness by getting an extra thirty minutes of vigorous exercise during the day, watching a funny video in the evening, doing a guided imagery exercise, and taking a warm bath before going to bed to insure that he gets a good night's sleep.

Julia is thirty-one-years old and an active mother of three. She has been diagnosed with lupus. She has learned that feeling overtired, having aches and pains, and seeing a rash on her face are early warning signs that her condition is worsening. By identifying these symptoms at this stage and responding to them by turning her household responsibilities over to another family member, doing progressive relaxation exercises three times during the day, engaging only in quiet activities with her children, journaling, and checking in with her doctor regarding possible medication changes, she can turn the situation around.

Many people have found that if they learn to become aware of these signs and take corrective action, they can return to feeling well instead of spiraling down into bad feelings and more severe symptoms and illness. In most cases, and with all kinds of symptoms and issues, addressing early warning signs is much easier, less stressful, and healthier than trying to deal with the situation after it has worsened.

This is a good time to talk to those who have been around when your symptoms have gotten worse. For example, Frank, a Vietnam War veteran with Post-Traumatic Stress Disorder, was able to talk to his family about the signs they noticed before he began a downward spiral. They had noticed that if he started having difficulty sleeping, ate only cereal and coffee, and became more withdrawn than was his usual nature, he was on the road to depression. By talking to those who had been around to see the whole process from beginning to end, he was able to gain valuable insight and information that proved to be very helpful to him in reducing the frequency and severity of relapse.

In this section you will make a list of early warning signs that alert you that your condition or situation might be worsening. You will then develop a plan of response to help keep the situation stabilized and hopefully reverse it so that you can go back to solely using your daily maintenance plan as a guide for daily living.

Write "Early Warning Signs" on the next tab in your binder. Photocopy the corresponding worksheets in the appendix and, once you have completed this section, recopy the exercise onto the photocopy and put it into your binder. You may want to ask family members, friends, and health care professionals to assist you in developing this list. They may have noticed some early warning signs that you haven't noticed. Some common early warning signs are as follows:

❏ anxiety

❏ forgetfulness

❏ lack of motivation

❏ avoiding doing things on daily maintenance list

❏ avoiding others or isolating yourself

❏ beginning irrational thought patterns

❏ feeling unconnected to your body

❏ increased negativity

❏ not keeping appointments

❏ feelings of discouragement, hopelessness

❏ nervousness

❏ inability to experience pleasure

❏ feeling slowed down or sped up

❏ spending money on unneeded items

❏ being obsessed with something that doesn't really matter

❏ feeling negative in general about people or the world

❏ increased irritability

❏ increased smoking

❏ being/feeling uncaring

❏ missing your intended exit when driving on the freeway

❏ substance abuse

❏ not answering the phone

❏ overeating

❏ feeling weepy

❏ feeling worthless, inadequate

❏ controlling and/or manipulative behaviors (try to be specific)

❏ easily frustrated

❏ not wanting to go out

❏ poor motor coordination with no physical reason

❏ feeling impulsive

❏ auras around lights

❏ dizziness

❏ excessive sweating

❏ headaches

❏ sore throat

❏ stuttering

❏ eruptions on the skin

❏ itching

❏ oily skin

❏ diarrhea

❏ mucus in the stools

❏ coughing

❏ stomach cramping

❏ incontinence

❏ dull ache in side (or other area of the body)

❏ blurred vision

❏ ringing ears

❏ clenched teeth

❏ failing to buckle your seat belt

❏ turning off the phone machine

❏ undereating

❏ compulsive behaviors

❏ being secretive

❏ feelings of abandonment or rejection

❏ don't want to move

❏ being too quiet

❏ feeling compelled to take too much pain medication

❏ craving drugs or alcohol

❏ aches and pains

❏ muscle cramping

❏ numbness or tingling

❏ earaches

❏ a raspy quality to your voice

❏ change in skin tone

❏ sores that won't heal

❏ dry skin

❏ nausea

❏ constipation

❏ a runny nose

❏ excessive sneezing

❏ abdominal rumbling

❏ lack of or lowered libido

❏ feeling of constriction in the throat

❏ hearing difficulties

❏ hearing voices

❏ tooth pain

❏ bleeding gums

❏ feeling of heaviness in the abdomen (or other part of the body)

❏ not being able to eat foods you
   usually can without experiencing
   stomach upset

❏ dry or itchy eyes

❏ heartburn

❏ having spots on the body that
   are tender or painful to the
   touch

Other early warning signs:

_____

_____

_____

_____

_____

    Every day, when you review your daily maintenance list, review this list so you become very familiar with your early warning signs and can respond quickly, before the situation worsens.

    Beth reviewed her early warning signs of both mood instability and fibromyalgia every day for four months. After that time, she noticed that she had memorized them and had become adept at recognizing these signs as soon as they appeared. For instance, excessive overeating was an early warning sign of depression for her. Before she began using WRAP, this overeating would go on for days before she realized that she was getting depressed. By that time she had usually gained some weight and upset her digestive system, and the depression had become more firmly entrenched. Now she recognizes overeating as an early warning sign on the first day it occurs and takes corrective action. She stops eating sugar, adjusts her diet so it includes root vegetables like carrots, winter squash, and potatoes to satisfy her cravings for food, spends an extra thirty minutes outdoors, has a daily peer counseling session, does one breathing awareness exercise every day, and spends an hour involved in an activity she enjoys.

    When you notice your own early warning signs, take action while you still can. Use the next pages to develop your response plan in case you begin to notice early warning signs. You may need more than one plan if you have more than one condition for which you are using WRAP. In my case, for example, I have developed two plans—one to use when I am experiencing early warning signs of fibromyalgia, and one to use when I am experiencing early warning signs of depression or mania. Use photocopies of the corresponding forms in the appendix if you have multiple conditions. In this part of the plan, you may want to make a distinction between things you must do when you recognize early warning signs and things you may choose to do if you want to or feel the situation warrants it. In the following list, check yes, no, or maybe for each of the actions; at the end of the list there is space for you to list other actions you may choose to take or actions you must take.

If you notice early warning signs, you will do the following things:

	yes	no	maybe
❏ Do the things on your daily maintenance plan whether you feel like it or not.	❏	❏	❏
❏ Tell a supporter/counselor how you're feeling and ask for their advice. Ask them to help you figure out how to take the action they suggest.	❏	❏	❏
❏ Get peer counseling at least once a day until early warning signs diminish.	❏	❏	❏
❏ Do at least one focusing exercise a day until early warning signs diminish.	❏	❏	❏
❏ Do at least three ten-minute relaxation exercises each day until early warning signs diminish.	❏	❏	❏
❏ Write in your journal for at least fifteen minutes each day until early warning signs diminish.	❏	❏	❏
❏ Spend at least one hour each day involved in an activity you enjoy.	❏	❏	❏
❏ Ask others to take over your household responsibilities for a day.	❏	❏	❏
❏ Go to (number) twelve-step meetings.	❏	❏	❏
❏ Check in with your physician or other health care professional.	❏	❏	❏
❏ Surround yourself with loving, affirming people.	❏	❏	❏
❏ Spend more time with your pet(s).	❏	❏	❏
❏ Pray or meditate.	❏	❏	❏
❏ Read a good book.	❏	❏	❏
❏ Dance, sing, listen to good music, or play a musical instrument.	❏	❏	❏
❏ Watch a comedic video.	❏	❏	❏
❏ Exercise.	❏	❏	❏
❏ Go fishing.	❏	❏	❏
❏ Go fly a kite.	❏	❏	❏

Things you *must* do when you recognize early warning signs:

_____

_____

_____

_____

_____

_____

Things you *may choose* to do when you recognize early warning signs:

_____

_____

_____

_____

_____

_____

You have now completed the "early warning signs" section of your WRAP. Give yourself credit for the good work you are doing for yourself and for those people who care about you.

Signs of Potential Crisis

When Things Are Breaking Down or Getting Worse

Sometimes in spite of your best efforts, your symptoms or circumstances may progress to the point where the situation has become very uncomfortable, serious, or even dangerous, but you are still able to take action on our own behalf. It may be that an illness has worsened, you may be suffering from an injury, or a very stressful, traumatic event may have occurred. The situation could develop slowly or suddenly. This is a very important time. It is necessary to take immediate action to turn the situation around and prevent a crisis or the need for help and intervention from others. At this time, more intensive, structured, and directive action is needed.

Responding when your symptoms, circumstances, or events have begun to further increase in severity is much more difficult. It takes courage, a basic sense of trust, and persistence. During these times it becomes very important to know how you recover and what you need to do to promote the healing process. The healing process is unique for each person. You need to recognize and honor *your* healing process and pace. Give yourself time to rest and heal. Involve yourself in restful activities like gardening, walking in the woods, looking at something beautiful, or working on a creative project. If possible, put off taking on new projects like looking for a new job, starting school, beginning a new treatment, or starting a new therapy. You may need to avoid things, people, and activities that are jarring, grating, wearing, or chaotic. Give yourself time to talk about your situation with people who are supportive and comfortable to be with. Take time for yourself and time to be alone. Recognize when you are becoming too tired, and respect your limits for physical, emotional, and mental stress. Following are several examples.

Susan suffered emotional and physical abuse as a child and a back injury as an adult, along with recurrent episodes of asthma and allergies. Her recovery has involved learning about and honoring her pace and stamina. It is slower than she would like it to be, but the consequences of overdoing worsen all her symptoms. She knows that if she is not careful, a hospitalization may result. She is able to accomplish all her goals if she prioritizes and allows flexibility so that if she needs extra rest she can get it. When something stressful happens in her life, she increases her support and takes time off from her job. She asks her friends to be patient with her as sometimes she would want to get together and sometimes needed time to be alone.

Paul has had severe diabetes for many years and knows that he has had a sharp rise in his blood sugar that needs immediate attention when he starts feeling dizzy. For him, this is a sign that things are very bad, but he can still take some action in his own behalf. He immediately lets someone know—in person if possible or by phone if he is alone. Then he gives himself insulin through an insulin pump.

For Lynn, experiencing pain that makes it hard for her to walk and do repetitive tasks lets her know she is in trouble. Her fibromyalgia is worsening. At this point, she knows she has to see her physician immediately, take a warm bath, arrange for a massage, ask family members to take over household responsibilities, and take at least two days off from work.

Identifying Symptoms of Potential Crisis

On the next tab in your binder, write "When Things are Breaking Down." Develop a list of signs, symptoms, and circumstances that would indicate to you that things are breaking down, or that the potential for a crisis is increasing. Do this by reviewing the following examples and adding other ideas of your own. These symptoms or signs vary from person to person. What may mean "things are breaking down" to one person may mean "crisis" to another, and may mean "early warning sign" for another person. Keep this in mind as you develop your list.

Some of the things on this list may be the same things you have put on your early warning signs list. The difference may be in intensity, duration, and the addition of other symptoms and signs that are appearing at the same time. Be as clear as possible in noting these things as a reminder to yourself and anyone who is supporting you as you use this plan. These things may be very clear now, when you are feeling well, but a written reminder will be very helpful when the situation is worsening and things become more confusing.

Choose from the following list any of the symptoms or situations which, for you, mean that things have worsened and are close to the crisis stage:

- ❑ an event that causes a strong grief reaction
- ❑ an event that causes severe stress for a long time
- ❑ irrational responses to the events and the actions of others
- ❑ unable to sleep for three days
- ❑ increased pain
- ❑ pain in specific areas of the body (specify where)
- ❑ lapses in memory
- ❑ numbness and tingling sensations
- ❑ avoiding eating, refusing to eat
- ❑ dissociation (blacking out, spacing out, losing time)
- ❑ thoughts of self-harm
- ❑ obsessed with negative thoughts
- ❑ excessive spending
- ❑ racing thoughts
- ❑ chain smoking
- ❑ substance abuse
- ❑ not feeling anything
- ❑ paranoia
- ❑ vomiting
- ❑ overeating junk food
- ❑ spending excessive amounts of money (specify how much that means for you)

- ❑ an event that causes long-term instability in your life
- ❑ feeling very oversensitive and fragile
- ❑ sleeping much more than usual (describe how much you mean)
- ❑ feeling very needy
- ❑ severe pain anywhere
- ❑ severe and debilitating headaches
- ❑ poor coordination
- ❑ hearing things that others can't hear
- ❑ wanting to be totally alone
- ❑ risk-taking behaviors (e.g. driving fast)
- ❑ substance abuse
- ❑ inability to slow down
- ❑ bizarre behaviors (be specific)
- ❑ seeing things that aren't there
- ❑ taking out anger on others
- ❑ food abuse
- ❑ suicidal thoughts
- ❑ bloody stools
- ❑ food bingeing
- ❑ fainting spells

Other signs of potential crisis:

_____

_____

_____

_____

_____

_____

Developing a Plan to Reduce Signs of Potential Crisis

Write a plan that you think will help reduce your signs and symptoms when they have progressed to this point. Refer to the following sample plan to develop your own plan. Transfer to your plan the activities that you feel would relieve your symptoms. The listings of times and length of involvement in activities are only examples. Change them to meet your needs.

On the forms provided, write a plan that you feel will help reduce your signs and symptoms when they have progressed to this point (in which you feel a crisis is impending). The plan now needs to be very directive with few choices and very clear instructions. Some of the responses you list may be the same as those listed for responding to triggers and early warning signs, but you may need to do them more often and/or for longer periods of time. Transfer to your plan the activities that you feel would relieve your symptoms, along with other ideas you have had and activities that have helped in the past.

Sample plan:

When things are breaking down, I need to do *all* of the following:

- call my doctor or other health care professional and arrange an appointment within the next twenty-four hours

- call and talk to my supporters as long as I need

- arrange for someone to stay with me and cook me healthy food until my symptoms subside

- make sure I am doing everything on my daily maintenance plan

- take at least three days off from any responsibilities

- have at least two peer counseling sessions daily

- do three deep breathing relaxation exercises

- do two focusing exercises

- write in my journal for at least thirty minutes

When things are breaking down, I may choose to do any of the following (after completing the required activities):

- creative activities

- watching funny videos

- exercise

- journaling

- yoga

- a warm bath

Your response plan for when things are breaking down (this form is duplicated in the appendix).

Signs of potential crisis:

_____

_____

_____

_____

_____

_____

Required responses to these signs

_____

_____

_____

_____

_____

_____

Optional responses to these signs:

_____

_____

_____

_____

_____

_____

Keeping Your Response Plan Current

Because your intervention at this point is so important in avoiding a crisis, review the plan after the hard time has passed. The following questions will guide you through this process (this form is duplicated in the appendix).

- Are there some symptoms or signs that should be added to your list? y _____ n _____ If so, what are they:

_____

_____

_____

_____

- Are there symptoms or signs that should be removed from your list? y _____ n _____ If so, what are they:

_____

_____

_____

_____

- Did your response plan work? y _____ n _____ If not, how could it be changed so that it would be more effective next time?

_____

_____

_____

_____

Return to your WRAP and make these changes. It's a good idea to review your symptom and response plan after each time your symptoms indicate things are breaking down and you have to use your response plan.

Chapter 4

Developing a Crisis Plan

In spite of your best planning and assertive action on your own behalf, your symptoms and signs may increase to the crisis level—a time when you need others to take over responsibility for your care and make decisions in your behalf.

Being in crisis is a difficult situation, one that no one likes to face. People in crisis feel as if they are completely out of control. Writing a crisis plan—when you are well—to instruct others about how to care for you when you are not well keeps you in control, even when it seems as if things are out of control. Often, when your symptoms worsen, family members and friends may waste time trying to figure out what to do. With a crisis plan they will know what to do, saving everyone time and frustration, and insuring that your needs will be met.

Marlie has been living with epilepsy that resulted from a brain injury in an accident. For her, it is a crisis situation when she has a seizure where she is unconscious for longer than two minutes. In this situation, others need to call her doctor immediately to report the situation, take precautions to keep her safe, and administer her medication as soon as she has been conscious for five minutes. If she is unconscious for more than five minutes, they need to give her a shot, which is ready for her, and call for transportation to the hospital. She has all of this clearly described in her crisis plan so others know exactly what to do.

A crisis plan needs to be developed when you are feeling well. However, you cannot do it quickly. Decisions like this take time and often collaboration with health care professionals, family members, and other supporters. I worked on developing my crisis plan with my counselor over a period of several months. As you proceed you may discover thoughts, ideas, and options that you had not previously considered.

Before you begin, I will share with you information and ideas that others have included on their crisis plans to help you in developing your crisis plan. As you note things that should be included in your plan, fill them in on the forms in this book.

On the next tab in your binder, write "Crisis Plan." After you have completed filling out the plan in this chapter, turn to the appendix, make a photocopy of the crisis plan worksheets provided, and transfer the information onto the photocopies. Then insert that version of your crisis plan into your binder.

Part 1: What I'm Like When I'm Feeling Well

The first step in this process is describing what you are like when you are well. Of course, your family and friends know what you are like (though when in distress, or after a long period in which you aren't feeling well, they may benefit from a reminder). But an emergency room doctor may think your ceaseless chatter is a sign of mania when you're just naturally talkative. Or perhaps you are usually quite introverted. An unsuspecting doctor may see this as depression. Complaints of severe pain may be ignored by health care professionals who don't realize that you are the kind of person who rarely complains about anything. Poor decision making or mistreatment could occur.

In the blank space that follows, write words or phrases that describe what you are like when you are well. You can use the list that you developed for your daily maintenance plan or develop a special list for your crisis plan. If you are developing a new list for your crisis plan, review the following suggestions and write down those that apply to you along with other descriptive words that you feel describe you well. It may be helpful to ask others for descriptive terms too, as you are trying to describe yourself from the outside in—how others see you when you are well.

When I am feeling well, I am:

- ❏ talkative
- ❏ outgoing
- ❏ adventurous
- ❏ outspoken
- ❏ shy
- ❏ wise-cracking
- ❏ quietly humorous
- ❏ practical outlook
- ❏ pale skinned
- ❏ flirtatious
- ❏ polite

- ❏ quiet
- ❏ withdrawn
- ❏ cautious
- ❏ easygoing
- ❏ intellectual
- ❏ humorous
- ❏ warm natured
- ❏ energetic
- ❏ rosy cheeked
- ❏ reserved
- ❏ interested in surroundings

❏ clean   ❏ neatly groomed

❏ casual looking

Other words that describe how you are when you're well:

_____

_____

_____

Part 2: Crisis Signs and Symptoms

In this section you will be describing those symptoms that would indicate to others that they need to take over responsibility for your care and make decisions in your behalf. You may find that this is the most difficult part of developing your crisis plan. This is hard for everyone. It is very difficult to envision a time when others would have to take over responsibility for you or your care. And yet, through careful, well-developed descriptions and plans, you stay in control even when things seem to be out of control.

Allow yourself plenty of time to complete this section. When you start to feel discouraged or daunted, set it aside for a while. Ask your friends, family members, and health care professionals for input. However, always remember that the final determination is up to you. It may take several months to complete this section. Try to look back at difficult times in the past and come up with a list of symptoms or indicators that will let others know that you are in a crisis and that you need them to take over for you.

In developing your list, be very clear in describing the symptoms or situation. Don't try to summarize. Use as many words as it takes. In other parts of your plan, it is you who are aware of your symptoms. In the crisis plan, a person close to you has to become aware of the symptoms or circumstances to take action on your behalf.

Use the following symptoms for ideas in developing your own list:

❏ unable to recognize family members and friends

❏ incorrectly identifying family and friends

❏ severe pain (describe specifics)

❏ unable to control bodily functions

❏ unable to move limbs

❏ extreme weakness in limbs

❏ slurred speech

❏ unable to speak

❏ high fever

- ❏ unusual skin tone

- ❏ unconscious or semi-conscious

- ❏ uncontrollable pacing, unable to stay still

- ❏ very rapid breathing or seeming to be gasping for breath

- ❏ severe agitation

- ❏ constant moving

- ❏ the inability to stop repeating very negative statements like "I want to die"

- ❏ inability to stop compulsive behaviors like constantly counting everything or washing

- ❏ catatonic, not moving for long periods of time

- ❏ neglecting personal hygiene (for how many days?)

- ❏ unable to care for myself (specify in what ways)

- ❏ not cooking or doing any housework (for how many days?)

- ❏ extreme mood swings daily

- ❏ destructive to property (throwing things, etc.)

- ❏ not understanding what people are saying

- ❏ thinking you are someone you aren't

- ❏ thinking you have the ability to do something you don't

- ❏ self-destructive behavior (specify, if possible)

- ❏ abusive or violent behavior

- ❏ criminal activities

- ❏ substance abuse

- ❏ threatening suicide or acting suicidal

- ❏ not getting out of bed at all

- ❏ refusing to eat or drink

- ❏ very groggy for a long period of time (how long?)

- ❏ loss of memory

- ❏ seizures

- ❏ consistently mixing up the order of words

Other symptoms:

_____

_____

_____

_____

_____

Part 3: Supporters

In the next section of the crisis plan, list those people who you want to take over if the symptoms or circumstances you described in the previous section of your crisis plan occur. They can be family members, friends, or health care professionals.

It's best to have at least five people on your list of supporters. If you have only one or two, they might not be available when you really need them (e.g., they might be on vacation, sick, or have a sick family member). If you don't have that many people who you think would be available to you in a time of crisis, you may need to work on developing new and closer relationships with people and expanding your support system by going to support groups, engaging in community activities, and volunteering. There is information on developing a support system in chapter 6.

Following are some examples of attributes you may want from those who you would like to take over and make decisions for you in the event of a crisis. Check off those that are important to you:

❑ responsible   ❑ honest

❑ sincere   ❑ knowledgeable

❑ calm   ❑ patient

❑ compassionate   ❑ understanding

❑ trustworthy   ❑ competent

❑ caring   ❑ innovative

List other attributes you would like from your supporters:

_____

_____

_____

You may want to name some people for certain tasks, like taking care of the children or paying the bills, and others for tasks like staying with you and taking you to health care appointments.

Name	Connection/Role	Phone Number	Specific Tasks

Also list your health care professionals, their phone numbers, and their role in your treatment and care; this will allow your supporters to contact them when necessary.

Physician _____ Phone Number _____

When to contact _____

Pharmacist _____ Phone Number _____

When to contact _____

Other health care professionals

Name _____ Phone Number _____

Specialty _____

When to contact _____

Name _____ Phone Number _____

Specialty _____

When to contact _____

Name _____   Phone Number _____

Specialty _____

When to contact _____

Name _____   Phone Number _____

Specialty _____

When to contact _____

There may be health care professionals or family members that might be contacted when you have a crisis that you *do not want involved* in making decisions for you or providing you with care (e.g., health care professionals or family members who made decisions that were not according to your wishes in the past) or they may be people who you feel are not capable of providing you with the kind of support you need. They could inadvertently get involved in your care if you don't specify that you don't want them involved.

I *do not* want the following people involved in any way in my care or treatment:

Name	**Why You Do Not Want Them Involved (optional)**

It's wise to include a section that describes how disputes or differences of opinion in interpreting this crisis plan are to be settled. You may want a majority of people listed in your plan to agree on a particular course of action, or you may want to name one of your supporters to make the final determination at such a time.

I want disputes between my supporters settled as follows:

_____

_____

_____

_____

_____

Part 4: Medication

Depending on the circumstances of the crisis, your supporters may need to work with your physician and other health care providers to make decisions about the use and choice of medications. To assist them in this process, you need to provide your supporters with information about medication commonly used to treat your condition. Copy the following form and fill one out for each medication you use and for those you feel might be considered if your condition worsens.

Questions to Ask the Doctor About Medication

generic name _____   product name _____

product category _____   suggested dosage level _____

How does this medication work? What do you expect it to do?

_____

_____

How long will it take to achieve that result? _____

What are the risks associated with taking this medication?

_____

_____

What kind of an effectiveness track record does this medication have?

_____

What short-term side effects does this medication have?

_____

_____

_____

What long-term side effects does this medication have?

_____

_____

_____

Is there any way to minimize the chances of experiencing these side effects? If so, what are they?

_____

_____

_____

Are there any dietary or lifestyle suggestions or restrictions when using this medication?

_____

_____

_____

_____

Why do you recommend this particular medication?

_____

_____

_____

_____

Have you had other patients that have used it? If so, how have they done?

_____

_____

_____

How is this medication monitored?

_____

_____

_____

What tests will I need prior to taking this medication?

_____

_____

How often will I need these tests while taking the medication?

_____

_____

What symptoms indicate that the dosage should be changed or the medication stopped?

_____

_____

_____

Your physician, in working with your supporters, may recommend a medication that you have not studied. Name a supporter or several supporters who could fill out this form for you, so that they have needed information to decide if the medication should be used.

Supporter to study recommended medications _____

List any allergies you have that would affect medication decisions:

_____

_____

_____

List the medications you are currently using, the dosage, why you are taking them, and other pertinent information.

Medication	Dosage	Purpose	Other Information

List those medications you would *prefer* to take if medications or additional medications became necessary, and explain why you would choose to use them.

Medication	Why I Prefer to Use This Medication

List those medications that would be *acceptable* to you if medications became necessary, and why you would choose them.

Medication	Why I Would Find This Medication Acceptable

List those medications that you *don't* want to use and give the reasons why.

Medication	Why I Don't Want to Use It

Part 5: Treatments

The treatment options for dealing with various health conditions and life situations are extensive. They continue to expand as health care professionals and researchers study ways to increase overall health and wellness. Everyone has preferences about those treatments they would prefer in crisis situations, and those they would want to avoid.

For instance, while using electroshock therapy to treat depression is very controversial, some people have found it to be helpful and would want to have this treatment again if they could no longer care for themselves. Others express fears about the treatment and possible long-term memory loss and other side effects. Another example would be that you may or may not want chemotherapy or radiation to treat cancer. Keep your supporters advised as you gather new information about treatment options by revising your crisis plan and giving them a copy. Read the following examples for ideas.

Sandy had been receiving radiation treatment for breast cancer. Because of the severe side effects, debilitating nausea and fatigue, which she felt further compromised her health, she has decided not to use radiation again if her cancer recurs. She put this in her crisis plan and distributed it to all of her supporters.

Bill has been trying for many years to deal with alcoholism, an addiction he has had good success in managing for the past year. Before that he had tried methadone treatment to address his problem with alcoholism. It didn't help, and it made him nauseous and confused. He has requested that, in the event of a crisis, it not be used in the future.

You may have also tried some alternative therapies (therapies that may not be well-recognized by the medical community) such as acupuncture, massage therapy, and/or homeopathy. Specify on your crisis plan which have helped, as well as those that have not. Also list alternative therapies you'd be willing to try in the event of a crisis, and those you would not.

Before you write your list of treatment preferences, and those you wish to avoid, you may want to do some research on treatments you have thought about using, that others have used, or that your physician or other health care professional have suggested might be used in an emergency. To get this information:

- ask your health care professionals (this may not be an unbiased source, so don't end your information search there)

- use your local library, or the medical library in a nearby hospital

- contact organizations that focus on treatment of the symptoms or situation about which you are concerned

- do a literature search of journal articles through a college or university library

- search the internet for pertinent information

- talk to others who are dealing with similar symptoms or issues

After you have reviewed all this information, you can decide whether or not this is a treatment you would want for yourself if you are in a crisis.

List your treatment preferences and those you want to avoid. Use the following list to remind yourself of possible options. As you become aware of new treatment options that feel right to you, add them to your crisis plan and give a revised copy to your supporters:

❏ electroshock therapy		❏ radiation
❏ chemotherapy		❏ physical therapy
❏ hydrotherapy		❏ acupuncture
❏ acupressure		❏ homeopathy
❏ massage		❏ physical therapy
❏ counseling or therapy		❏ a support or twelve-step group

❏ cold or ice packs   ❏ hot packs

❏ hypnosis   ❏ surgery

Other treatments you'd be willing to try in the event of a crisis:

_____

_____

_____

Treatments you *wouldn't* be willing to try in the event of a crisis:

_____

_____

_____

Keep this list updated as your condition, circumstances, and preferences change.

Part 6: Options for Short-term and Long-term Care

In the past, crises, particularly a medical or psychiatric crisis, meant either short-term or long-term hospitalization. In these days of managed care systems, with the emphasis on prevention and home care, hospitalization has become a last resort, and the length of hospital stays has become shorter and shorter. While many people feel this trend is compromising their health, others are delighted to discover that there are ways to get optimal care while avoiding the inconvenience, separation from supporters, unfamiliar surroundings, and the high cost of hospital care. A friend recently told me that her doctor told her that shorter hospital stays benefit the patient more, and called hospitals "unhealthy places." While that may be an overstatement, it is certain that most of us are more comfortable resting and recuperating at home.

Many people are setting up plans so that they can stay at home and still get the care they need if they are in a crisis. This entire crisis plan will provide supporters and health care professionals with a guide to help them in arranging that for you. However, you can make it even easier by clearly describing exactly how you would like this "hospital at home" situation to be set up by instructing them on things like:

• the health care professionals who would need to be consulted

• the kinds of activities you would want to be involved in

• the kind of food you would want to eat and when you would want to eat it

• what you can easily do for yourself

In order to do this effectively, especially if you need around-the-clock care and/or constant observation and supervision, you need at least five friends or supporters, preferably more, who can take turns providing you with care. I have heard people say, "I don't need five people. My husband (mother, sister, daughter, best friend) will take care of me." In my view this is not a good idea. It burns people out and doesn't give them an opportunity to take care of themselves. With five or more people taking turns, nobody gets burned out or feels overwhelmed. These may be the same people who you named as your supporters in part 3 of this crisis plan, or it may include some additional people. For example, while many of the members of my women's support group are not on my support list, they are glad to come and take turns providing me with care when necessary.

When you are setting up this home care option in your crisis plan, it helps to name one or two people who can act as care-team leaders. Care-team leaders contact the people you have asked to provide you with care, schedule the times when they can provide care, and inform them of any special circumstances that might not be included in your plan, such as needing to be taken to an appointment with a health care professional, needing to be given medications at certain time, picking up medications at the pharmacy, or picking up a selection of videos.

An additional benefit of having at least five people working together to provide you with home care is that there are more people available to confer about decisions, increasing the chance that good decisions will be made on your behalf.

If I need home care, the following person/people have agreed to act as care-team leaders:

_____

_____

_____

_____

The following people have agreed to help provide me with home care in the event of a crisis.

Name	Phone Number	Availability Information (e.g., nights only)

These people would provide you with care as instructed by the team leader and according to the information contained in other parts of this plan, especially part 8.

Check out any home care services, such as home health aides and visiting nurses, who might be able to help. There are even some doctors who still do house calls. Rescue and emergency care personnel might need to be advised in advance if there is a chance your condition could become life threatening; doing this could result in saving precious minutes. In addition, there may be programs in your community that could provide you with part-time care or respite care in the event of certain kinds of health care emergencies. Check these out, and if any might be possibilities for you, include information about the services they provide and share this information with your supporters.

Home care services to
contact if necessary: Phone   Services

_____

_____

_____

Doctor(s) who may be willing to make a house call: Phone

_____

_____

_____

Rescue personnel to be advised in
case my condition becomes life threatening: Phone

_____

_____

_____

Community care and/or
respite programs: Phone   When to Be Used

_____

_____

_____

Part 7: Hospital Care

While hospitalization use is decreasing rapidly, your condition may necessitate either short-term or longer hospital care to:

- provide you with professional care
- closely monitor your condition and respond quickly when necessary, especially after invasive treatments like surgery
- provide treatment and other needed interventions
- keep you safe
- provide care if your supporters are not able to provide you with the home care

Using your personal experience with hospital facilities and information you have learned through your own research, list those hospitals where you would prefer to be hospitalized if necessary and those you wish to avoid. If hospitalization is likely or is scheduled (for certain treatments or surgery), and there are several hospital options, you may want to visit the facility prior to your stay there.

In the process of determining those facilities where you would prefer to be hospitalized if hospitalization became necessary, it may help you to think about the attributes you would want in a treatment facility. I would prefer a hospital that is:

- a place that is conducive to healing
- able to provide exceptional medical and/or other kinds of care
- user friendly
- amenable to having both my family and myself involved in decisions about my care
- willing to keep me in the hospital as long as necessary for my particular condition
- known for its personalized care
- staffed with doctors who specialize in certain kinds of treatments and/or conditions
- staffed with a treatment team that will work together to explore my options
- well-staffed with highly qualified professionals
- knowledgeable about alternative therapies
- located in/away from a metropolitan area
- known for its cleanliness
- known for its attention to details of comfort
- known for its high quality care

- known for its personalized service

- known for its up-to-date options

- intent on minimizing use of medications and invasive treatments

- known for its proper use of medications and treatments

- equipped with staff who are competent

- known for its caring staff

- staffed with health care professionals with good bedside manners

- not known for denying service based on lack of funds

- known for its high quality food with special dietary options (e.g., kosher, vegetarian)

- private

- quiet

- fair about friends and family having adequate visiting opportunities at reasonable hours

- willing to give me the freedom to be up and around as much as possible

- in an area that provides good views out the windows

- willing to make available activities such as books on loan, libraries, VCRs

- comfortable and has a pleasant atmosphere

Other attributes that are important to you in choosing a hospital facility:

_____

_____

_____

_____

_____

Using your prior visits and the above list as a guide, complete the following chart.

If I need hospitalization or treatment in a treatment facility, I prefer the following facilities in order of preference:

Name	Contact Person	Phone Number

I prefer this facility because:

_____

_____

_____

Name   **Contact Person**   **Phone Number**

_____

I prefer this facility because:

_____

_____

_____

Name   **Contact Person**   **Phone Number**

_____

I prefer this facility because:

_____

_____

_____

Name   **Contact Person**   **Phone Number**

_____

I prefer this facility because:

_____

_____

_____

Avoid using the following hospital or treatment facilities:

Name   **Reason to avoid using**

_____

_____

_____

Part 8: Help from Others

This is the part of the plan that makes the whole plan work. Develop it carefully. Give it a lot of thought. Think about past experiences. Ask family members, friends, and health care professionals for input. Avoid summarizing. In difficult times, supporters appreciate as much information as possible, and won't want to waste time trying to figure out what you are trying to tell them.

Describe in as much detail as possible:

- what you anticipate needing from others in the event of a crisis
- interventions that have helped in the past
- interventions that you think might help
- specific tasks for specific people
- interventions or actions that should be avoided

What you need your supporters to do for you that would help reduce symptoms and keep you safe (check any that apply):

❑ listen to you without giving you advice, judging you, or criticizing you

❑ hold you

❑ let you pace

❑ encourage you to move, help you move

❑ lead you through a relaxation or stress reduction exercise

❑ peer counsel with you

❑ take you for a walk

❑ provide you with materials so you can draw, paint, sculpt, etc.

❑ give you the space to express your feelings

❑ don't talk to you

❑ talk to you

❑ encourage you

❑ reassure you

❑ feed you good food (give suggestions on foods that make you feel good—you may also want to list foods to avoid)

❑ make sure you get exposure to outdoor light for at least thirty minutes daily

❑ play you comedic videos (list favorites)

❑ play you music (list favorites)

❑ just let you rest

❏ keep you from hurting myself, even if that means they have to restrain you or get help from others

❏ keep you from being abusive to or hurting others no matter what they need to do to accomplish this

❏ rub your back

❏ put hot or cold packs on you (specify hot or cold, where on your body to apply, how long to apply, how often to apply, and where the materials are in your house)

❏ arrange for a massage (give specifics so they can call your massage therapist—include name and phone number—and make an appointment for an office or home visit)

❏ help you to do as much as you can for yourself

❏ reorient you if you can't figure out where or who you are

Other things you need your supporters to do for you to help reduce symptoms and keep you safe:

_____

_____

_____

_____

_____

_____

Possible tasks you may need others to do for you include:

❏ buy groceries

❏ pay bills (include information on where to find them)

❏ take care of the children

❏ take care of the pets

❏ water the plants

❏ contact employers (include information on what you want employers to be told)

❏ take over work-related tasks

❏   contact family members and friends (include information on exactly who should be told and what they should be told)

❏   cancel or reschedule appointments

❏   take care of home maintenance tasks (i.e., clean and organize the house)

❏   do the laundry

❏   do vehicle maintenance tasks

Make a list of tasks that you will need others to do for you during this difficult time. You can use the following format:

Things you need others to do for you.	**Who you want to do it.**

In trying to be helpful, supporters may decide to take some actions in your behalf that would really be harmful, make you feel worse, or worsen the situation. Through your past experience you have probably discovered what some of those things are. List them in your plan. Some examples include:

❏   forcing you to do anything

❏   offering advice more than once a day

❏   chattering

❏   getting angry with you

❏   impatience

❏   trying to talk you into things

❏   playing certain kinds of music (name them)

❏   trying to entertain you

❏   guilt trips

❏   invalidation

❏ not listening to you   ❏   threats

❏ playing certain videos (name   ❏   blaming or shaming
   them)

Things that would not help or might even worsen your symptoms:

_____

_____

_____

_____

_____

_____

_____

_____

Part 9: When Your Supporters No Longer Need to Use This Plan

You will get better, and your supporters will no longer need to follow this plan to keep you safe. Make a list of indicators that let your supporters know that they no longer need to follow this plan. Some examples include:

❏ when you have slept through the night for three nights

❏ when you eat at least two good meals a day

❏ when you are taking care of your own personal hygiene needs

❏ when you can carry on a good conversation

❏ when you keep your living space organized

❏ when you can be in a crowd without becoming anxious

Your supporters no longer need to take care of you when:

_____

_____

_____

_____

When you have finished your crisis plan, ask one or several supporters to review it to see if they understand it or feel they need additional information. Revise your plan according to their input if necessary.

While the legality of these documents differs from state to state, it is still the best assurance that, in the event of a crisis, your wishes will be carried out by your supporters as you have directed. You can help assure that your crisis plan will be followed by signing it in the presence of two witnesses and having it notarized. You can also appoint a person as durable power of attorney, responsible for seeing that the crisis plan is followed as closely as possible. Contact a lawyer if you are concerned about the legality of your document. If your resources are limited, contact the legal aid services in your area.

Give each supporter a copy of your crisis plan. Give them a new copy of the plan each time you update it. Review it with them each time you give them a copy so that they are clear about your intent.

Once you have completed and distributed your crisis plan, put a copy in your binder. Update it when you learn new information or change your mind about things. Give your supporters new copies of your crisis plan each time you revise it.

To facilitate effective implementation of your crisis plan and to help your supporters more easily work together, you might consider having a meeting of your supporters. A friend of mine set up a potluck dinner for her supporters. After dinner they discussed how they would work together if the crisis plan needed to be implemented. Another woman treated all of her supporters to lunch at a local restaurant to discuss the plan.

You may want to use the form in the appendix to develop your crisis plan. If you want to adapt the form to meet your personal needs and preferences, you can make a copy on your computer and fill it in that way. Doing this will also facilitate the process of making regular changes.

Chapter 5

Establishing a Nurturing Lifestyle

Your Wellness Toolbox

Chapters 5–8 cover a variety of tools to use to respond to any symptoms, unhealthy situations, and uncomfortable or dangerous feelings. Review them. Try them. Figure out which ones would work well for you. Many of these are named in the list that appears both at the end of chapter 3 and in the appendix. As you read chapters 5–8, you may want to use the corresponding list in the appendix (called Wellness Toolbox Checklist) to check off those tools that you want to use in your WRAP, as well as list other tools you wish to use that aren't mentioned on the list.

Healthy Lifestyle Choices

You may have been trying for a long time to get a handle on lifestyle issues. These issues may have been a source of stress for a long time. For example, Sherri knew she was very unhappy. Her life was hectic and chaotic. She didn't exercise. She primarily ate fast food and was always on the run. Diagnosis with a life-threatening illness provided her with the impetus for beginning to use WRAP and making changes that have literally saved her life.

Educate Yourself

You may find that there are times when you will need more information about the specific illness, problem, or issue you are addressing in your WRAP process. You can include this in your WRAP. For instance, Sam knows he needs more education about his diabetes when he has trouble keeping his blood sugar in the right range.

This research might include:

❑ reviewing your own writings, files, and home library

❑ searching the internet

❑ research at the library

❑ attending an educational support group, workshop, or lecture

Exercise

Exercise is a great response to many difficult symptoms and circumstances. Exercise helps reduce unpleasant symptoms, improves your overall stamina and health, and helps in reducing stress. The right exercise can even be fun. The benefits of exercise include:

❑ an overall feeling of well-being

❑ enhanced ability to sleep the recommended amount of time, with more restful sleep

❑ improved memory and ability to concentrate

❑ decrease in some uncomfortable symptoms

❑ decreased irritability and anxiety

❑ improved self-esteem

❑ weight loss

❑ improved muscle tone

❑ increased endurance

❑ increased mobility

I have discovered that my daily walks provide me with the added benefit of getting me outdoors to help me feel part of the natural world. Your exercise needs to be tailored to meet your specific needs. With some illnesses or disabilities, your ability to exercise may be limited or restricted in some way. You may only be able to exercise for short periods of time. You may need to avoid strenuous activities. You may only be able to exercise some parts of your body. You may need to avoid moving some parts of you body. Talk to your health care providers about establishing a healthy exercise regimen that fits your specific needs. Keep your limitations, restrictions, and benefits in mind when incorporating exercise into your WRAP.

Exercise options continue to increase. Many people choose to exercise at a fitness center where working out along with others provides incentive. However, exercise doesn't need to be costly. Inexpensive or free recreational activities will suffice. Almost everyone can find an activity that suits them. It may be using exercise equipment at a gym or lifting weights at home. It may be swimming in a pool or hiking in the back country. The trick is to find something that appeals to you. You may want to consider some of the following options:

❏ walking   ❏ swimming

❏ skiing   ❏ skating

❏ running   ❏ hiking

❏ cycling   ❏ lifting weights

❏ aerobics   ❏ yoga

❏ gardening   ❏ splitting and stacking wood

❏ mowing the lawn   ❏ shoveling snow

❏ raking leaves   ❏ shooting hoops

❏ competitive sports   ❏ roller-blading

Some people love to exercise, and that is a reward in itself. Others find exercise tedious and boring, but they know it is good for them. Combining exercise with another activity, like walking with a friend, may help. Some people read or watch television while walking on their treadmill or using an exercise bicycle. Finding an exercise system that is rewarding and enjoyable can help keep you going.

It is often difficult to exercise when you are not feeling well. Remember, even a few minutes of moving will help. Do the best you can. If you can't do it at all right now, don't give yourself a hard time. Begin as soon as you start to feel a bit better. Listening to music while you exercise may help you feel more energized.

You can do the same kind of exercise every day or vary it—according to the weather, what you feel like, and what things you need to get done. If you haven't exercised recently or have health problems that may affect your ability to exercise, check with your physician before beginning an exercise program.

Diet

Developing your WRAP is an excellent way to change bad dietary habits or to incorporate recommended or preferred dietary habits into your life. In some instances, creating dietary change may be necessary to save your life. This was the case for Jill, twenty-five, who had been struggling to overcome a tendency toward anorexia that had plagued her since her midteens. She was well aware of the possible devastating consequences that could result from lack of proper nutrition. She has to fight against the insidious negative messages she tells herself: that she is too fat, that she should avoid food. She has developed plans that include minimum amounts and kinds of food that must be eaten everyday, along with corrective response strategies to use when her tendency to avoid food is on the increase. Her crisis plan alerts others to take over when she hasn't eaten anything in a day. She asks her supporters to arrange a session for her with her counselor. Her crisis plan also tells her supporters what kinds of foods are generally most appealing to her.

Frank's problem is the opposite of Jill's. Frank loves to eat. He especially enjoys eating red meats and rich desserts. A recent visit to the doctor has convinced him that he must take action. His "bad" cholesterol level is over three hundred, he is seventy-five pounds overweight, and he is beginning to have signs of heart disease. His WRAP plan includes avoiding certain foods and limiting his intake of other foods, along with eating more of some other kinds of foods. His WRAP also includes reminders to exercise and use relaxation strategies. He has developed a strong daily maintenance plan that includes exercise, three healthy meals, and time to relax. He knows he is triggered to indulge when he eats at certain restaurants. Because he doesn't want to avoid these restaurants, he has identified foods he can eat while he is there that are healthy, and when he orders his meal he always asks his server not to bring the dessert tray. If he is going to the restaurant with family members or friends, he asks them to either refrain from ordering dessert or understand when he excuses himself to take a walk when others eat dessert. He knows that eating a bag of potato chips is an early warning sign for him, a sign that he has to do something nice for himself and share his resolve to stick to his diet with a close friend. If Frank eats a rich dessert, he feels that things are breaking down. At this point, he knows he needs to reach out for the support of family members and friends to get him back on the right track. Frank says a crisis for him would be if he went totally off his diet for a full day or if he experienced shortness of breath and/or chest pain. His crisis plan tells others what to do if this happens.

You may begin to notice that uncomfortable symptoms begin or increase after you have eaten certain foods. The most common "bad guys" are sugar, caffeine, heavily salted foods, and fatty foods. Become aware of what you eat. Notice how you feel one half hour or more after you have eaten that food. If you notice you don't feel very good after eating a certain food, try eliminating it from your diet. If you feel better when you are no longer eating this food, you may want to include avoiding this and other foods that worsen your symptoms or situation in your WRAP. You may want to consult with a nutritionist to discover foods that will enhance your wellness. They can also guide you in foods to increase or avoid for help with your specific condition.

Determining what kind of a diet is best for you is a decision you need to make for yourself— hopefully in consultation with your health care provider or a nutritionist. Following are some general guidelines that are safe and that you can try right away:

- Focus your diet on natural and fresh foods as much as possible. Try to eat at least five servings of vegetables each day along with one or more servings of fresh fruit. Health food stores, food cooperatives, farmers' markets, and specialty supermarkets are often good sources of fresh, organic foods. While it may seem that these foods are more expensive, when you choose them instead of junk foods the increase in your food bill may be hardly noticeable.

- Avoid those foods that are high in processed flours (i.e., donuts, cookies, and cake), fat, sugar, salt, and food additives (i.e., MSG, BHT, BHA, and food colorings). Read the labels. If sugar is a main ingredient, along with processed flours, salt, and lots of words you can't pronounce, put it back on the shelf. Note that sugar may be "disguised" on the label as some other word that ends in "ose" (i.e., dextrose, lactose, or glucose). Salt is indicated by the word "sodium".

- If you feel gaseous, bloated, or very sleepy after you eat, you may benefit from drastically reducing or avoiding the sugar in your diet. The amount of sugar we eat in our society has increased substantially in the last century. Years ago a piece of sugar was a very special treat. Now we find sugar added to almost everything we eat, and our bodies don't know what to do with it.

- Reduce your intake of coffee, black teas, other caffeinated beverages, and chocolate (caffeine is known to cause anxiety and worry). Don't cut down on caffeine all at once. Reduce it slowly or you may develop flu-like symptoms and be quite grouchy.

- Have a rule for yourself that you will always be sitting down at the table when you are eating. Put on some quiet music and candles. If you live with others, tell them you are trying to have calmer mealtimes and work with them to develop a rule that prohibits arguing or discussion of "loaded" topics at mealtime. You may want to refrain from answering the phone at mealtimes, too.

- Eat only as much food as you need to feel satisfied. Don't stuff yourself. Make it a habit to eat three healthy meals a day with several healthy between meal snacks if desired. Don't skip any meals.

- If you are often too tired to cook after a busy day, or nothing in the house appeals to you, do some thoughtful grocery shopping. Buy a supply of healthy foods that you enjoy. Include foods that are easy to prepare. There are some healthy frozen dinners that you can have on hand for those days when you are exhausted.

- There are many excellent resource books, cookbooks, and magazines that can help you learn more about good nutrition and guide you in changing your food habits. Most libraries have a section of books that deal with food and nutrition. It helps enormously in changing eating habits to have recipes that you really like. Try not to make yourself eat foods you don't care for, or you may quickly abandon the new diet. Challenge yourself to try new foods.

- Set reasonable goals for creating changes in eating habits. Reward yourself with a nonfood treat each time you reach a goal. It might be a flower, a book or tape you have been wanting, an article of clothing, a trip to the movies, or time off from other responsibilities.

Light

Have you noticed that you feel worse in the fall and winter or when there are several cloudy days in a row? If you answered yes to these questions and check off several of the following symptoms, you may have seasonal affective disorder (more commonly known as SAD). If so, you may have to address the issue of getting enough exposure to outside light in your Wellness Recovery Action Plan. You will want to include spending time outdoors each day in your plan and even the use of a supplemental light source. Do you notice the following symptoms:

❑ lack energy

❑ want to sleep a lot

❑ have difficulty getting out of bed in the morning

❑ feel impatient with yourself and others

❑ crave sweets and junk food

❑ have difficulty being creative

❑ have difficulty concentrating and focusing your attention

❑ have difficulty getting motivated to do anything

❑ can't get as much done as usual

More people who live in the north (or in the southern regions of the southern hemisphere) have SAD than those who live closer to the equator. If you live in the north, it is even more likely that SAD or lack of light through the eyes is an issue for you. In the winter, the days are much shorter. You may get up and go to school or work in the dark and then come home after dark. Sometimes you may not get out in the daylight at all. Scientists have found that exposure to sunlight through the eyes helps some people feel better, as it affects the activity of neurotransmitters in the brain.

About ten years ago, Jacob's doctor suggested he try light therapy as a way of dealing with recurrent episodes of winter depression. He was skeptical, so he attended a workshop on light therapy that was led by a physician who had studied the effects of increased exposure to outdoor light, the use of supplemental full-spectrum lighting, and the use of specially designed light boxes. Jacob was intrigued. According to the physician's instruction, he tried light therapy by purchasing a shop light fixture and replacing the fluorescent bulbs with full spectrum bulbs. Jacob set it on the table in the room where he worked and voila!, he felt better. So he purchased two more shop light fixtures, again replaced the bulbs, and mounted the three light fixtures on a piece of plywood. He now had a rather primitive light box, and he began noticing a substantive difference. Since then, he has purchased a light box because it is more portable. It provides the light in his office through the winter and on cloudy days. Exposure to outdoor light or his light box is now part of Jacob's daily maintenance plan in the "Do I need to . . ." section. If he starts to experience early warning signs of depression, he increases his exposure to light. If he is having racing thoughts and feeling anxious, he reduces his exposure to light.

If you think you might have SAD, tell your doctor. He or she may be able to give you information on how to treat this disorder. If your doctors doesn't know very much about it, ask him or her to refer you to a doctor who does. A physician who knows about light therapy will help:

- diagnose whether you have SAD

- make sure light therapy is appropriate and there are no other medical conditions that need treatment

- work with you to develop treatment that fits your schedule and lifestyle

- help you in monitoring how you are doing

- provide additional ideas on how you can get more light

- give you needed encouragement and support

There are some simple, safe, effective things that you can do to help yourself feel better if you have SAD:

- Spend at least a half hour outside each day, even on cloudy days. If you are at school or work, try to spend some time outside during your lunch hour. Glasses, sunglasses, or contact lenses will block some of the sunlight you need. If you can't see well enough to go for a walk or be involved in some other outdoor activity without them, sit on a bench eating your lunch or talking to a friend.

- Gazing at the sky helps, but never look directly at the sun. The amount of light you get outside is enhanced by reflection off of snow and reduced by reflection off dark objects such as buildings and trees.

- Keep your indoor space well lit. Have plenty of lights on. Let in as much outdoor light as possible. Spend as much time as you can in spaces near windows in which the sun is coming through. While the window panes reduce by one half the beneficial light you are getting, it is still preferable to being in a room where there is no outdoor light.

- Consider using a specially made light box. Your doctor or pharmacist can tell you where to purchase one.

Some people notice almost immediate relief of symptoms when they begin increasing the amount of light they get through their eyes. It usually takes from four to five days to work, but may take up to two weeks. If you don't feel any better after two weeks of treatment with light therapy, your problem is probably not SAD-related.

Note: Tanning booths, which only shed light on the skin, are not recommended for light therapy. For more information on seasonal affective disorder, refer to the Resources section at the back of the book.

Sleep

Sleep problems can cause or worsen other symptoms or situations. Do you have any of the following sleep problems?

❏ You never seem to get to bed at a reasonable hour.

❑ You sleep much less than the recommended eight hours per night.

❑ You sleep much more than the recommended eight hours per night.

❑ You have a very hard time getting up in the morning.

❑ Sometimes you don't bother getting up in the morning.

❑ You have a hard time falling asleep once you are in bed.

❑ You awaken often during the night; sometimes or often you have a hard time getting back to sleep once you're awake.

❑ You wake up very early and have a hard time getting to sleep or can't get back to sleep.

❑ You often have nights where you sleep very little or don't sleep at all.

❑ You are kept awake by pain, worry, anxiety, and other symptoms.

Julie uses her WRAP to address her long-term problems with falling asleep at night. Although she was often very tired before she went to bed, she had a hard time falling asleep. Often she lay in bed for two to three hours before finally falling asleep. While her job performance was excellent when she slept well, when she didn't she was groggy, forgetful, and had a hard time focusing. She often skipped her exercise routine or other good things she could do for herself because she was feeling tired, choosing instead more sedentary activities. As a result, she found that she was putting on weight and napping often in the daytime. To reverse this situation, Julie discussed it with her doctor. He suggested some herbal remedies that she could use when sleep was difficult, a daily calcium supplement, magnesium supplements, and a prescription sleep medication for use when nothing else worked and her sleeping time had been shortened for several nights. In addition, she built into her WRAP some daily bedtime rituals, regular relaxation and stress reduction exercise, daily journaling, and weekly peer counseling sessions, along with the exercise and creative activities she had been neglecting.

If you are having sleep problems, it is a good idea to check in with your doctor. It is essential to see your doctor if:

❑ You awaken during the night gasping for breath.

❑ Your partner reports that you stop breathing as long as thirty seconds several times during the night.

❑ You snore loudly.

❑ You wake up feeling like you haven't been asleep.

❑ You often fall asleep during the day.

The following ideas, along with the resources listed in the back of this book, may help you address sleep related issues in your plans:

- Go to bed at the same time every night, and get up at the same time every morning. If you get to bed later than usual, get up at the same time anyway. You can take a short nap later in the day.

- Avoid naps that are longer than twenty minutes.

- Avoid "sleeping in" (sleeping much later than your usual time for getting up). It will make you feel worse.

- Avoid or limit the amount of caffeine in your diet. Coffee and tea are not the only culprits. There is enough caffeine in chocolate, some soft drinks, and some pain killers to interfere with sleep.

- Avoid the use of nicotine. It is a stimulant. If you cannot give up smoking right now, avoid smoking two to three hours before bedtime.

- Avoid the use of alcohol. While it may help you fall asleep, it will disturb your sleep later and may cause you to awaken early.

- Eat on a regular schedule and avoid eating a heavy meal prior to going to bed. Don't skip any meals.

- Eat plenty of dairy foods and dark green leafy vegetables. They contain calcium that helps you sleep. If you can't eat dairy foods, talk to your doctor about calcium supplementation.

- Exercise daily, but avoid strenuous or invigorating activity before going to bed.

- When you are trying to get to sleep, play soothing music on a tape or disc that shuts off automatically.

- Focus your attention on your breathing and silently repeat the words "in" as you inhale and "out" as you exhale.

- Read a nonstimulating book or watch a calm television program before going to bed.

- Write in your journal about anything and everything until you feel too tired to write anymore.

- Eating a turkey sandwich and a glass of milk before bedtime raises your serotonin level (a neurotransmitter) and makes you drowsy.

You may wake up in the middle of the night because you are hungry. Try having a small snack before you go to bed, something like a piece of fruit and a piece of cheese or some cottage cheese. You may want to try having a similar small snack if you awaken in the middle of the night. Other ways to aid sleep include:

- A warm bath or shower before going to bed may help you sleep.

- Check your local health food store for sleep enhancing herbs, amino acids, and homeopathic preparations that may help you get a good night's sleep.

- A drop of lavender oil on your pillow is relaxing and can help induce sleep.

- Drink a cup of herbal chamomile tea or take several chamomile capsules before going to bed.

- If menopausal symptoms such as hot flashes and night sweats are interfering with your sleep, see your health care professional for hormonal or herbal aids.

A woman at one of my workshops said, "I put myself to sleep by telling myself a story. It's usually a story I remember from my childhood. It keeps me from thinking about other things and worrying."

Daily Planning

Some people have found it helpful to develop "generic" daily plans—a nurturing plan that you can put into place any time you are not feeling well (physically or emotionally). They are especially helpful for those days when you can't figure out what to do next—a feeling that is common when symptoms are severe or you are having a hard time with the circumstances of your life. Your daily plan tells you exactly what to do. These plans can be used as part of your response plan to early warning signs and crises. They can be inserted in the section or sections of your personal action plans where they will be used.

These plans are best described by example. The following plan was developed by Susan, a fifty-five-year-old woman, to use when her symptoms of fibromyalgia become severe. In this circumstance, she experiences severe pain all over her body. Her mobility is limited as is her ability to perform certain daily tasks for herself. She is a high school teacher, but when her symptoms are this severe, she cannot work. She lives with her husband and an adult son.

7:00–8:00 A.M. Get up. Take a warm bath. Dress in green sweatsuit. Eat breakfast (bagel with cream cheese and piece of fruit) while boiling clay packs. Take medications and food supplements. Prepare a cup of herbal tea.

8:00–9:00 A.M. Sit in lounge chair with clay packs, wrapped in towels, on legs and neck. Drink tea. Call a friend to arrange a ride to physical therapy and for an afternoon visit. Read.

9:00–10:00 A.M. Journal writing or work on some other creative project.

10:00–11:00 A.M. Relaxation exercise with tape.

11:00–12:00 NOON. Call and talk to a supportive friend from the FMS support group. Do a focusing exercise.

12:00–1:00 P.M. Have tuna sandwich and piece of fruit for lunch while listening to folk music. Sit in lounge chair with clay packs wrapped in towels around legs and neck.

2:00–4:00 P.M. Go to physical therapy.

4:00–5:00 P.M. Peer counseling.

5:00–6:00 P.M. Talk with family members as they arrive home. Plan evening with them (who will make dinner, what will they cook).

6:00–7:00 P.M. Dinner with family.

7:00–9:00 P.M. Watch a video (have a family member pick one up) while using clay packs.

9:00–10:00 P.M. Take a warm bath. Read.

10:00 P.M. Go to bed.

Jeff has had problems with recurring deep depressions all his life. He is using WRAP to prevent further episodes and maintain his wellness. When things are breaking down, he knows he has to take at least one day off from his job as an auto mechanic and follow his generic plan. Jeff lives alone but has developed a strong circle of supportive friends.

7:00–8:00 A.M. Get up. Dress in casual clothing. Do ten minutes of stretching exercises. Walk for thirty minutes. Take a shower. Dress in jeans and cotton shirt.

8:00–9:00 A.M. Prepare scrambled eggs with ham, whole grain toast, and orange juice for breakfast. Eat breakfast while listening to jazz. Arrange support for afternoon peer counseling and evening activities.

9:00–10:00 A.M. Call and talk to a friend while doing a load of laundry. Hang out the laundry. Do some housecleaning.

10:00–11:00 A.M. Work in the garden.

11:00-12:00 NOON. Do a relaxation exercise with tape followed by a focusing exercise.

12:00–1:00 P.M. Have a bowl of soup, a cheese sandwich, and a piece of fruit for lunch while listening to favorite music.

1:00–2:00 P.M. Journal writing. Work on a creative project.

2:00–3:00 P.M. Reading.

3:00–4:00 P.M. Bicycle ride.

4:00–5:00 P.M. Peer counseling with friend as arranged this morning.

5:00–7:00 P.M. Go out to dinner with a friend.

7:00–8:00 P.M. Watch favorite British comedies on television with friend.

8:00–9:00 P.M. Phone calls to family members and friends.

9:00–10:00 P.M. Take a warm bath. Read.

10:00 P.M. Go to bed.

Use the following space to develop a generic daily plan that you could use when you are having a hard time. A duplicate form can be found in the appendix.

Daily Planning Form

7:00–8:00 A.M.

_____

_____

8:00–9:00 A.M.

_____

_____

9:00–10:00 A.M.

_____

_____

10:00–11:00 A.M.

_____

_____

11:00–12:00 NOON

_____

_____

12:00–1:00 P.M.

_____

_____

1:00–2:00 P.M.

_____

_____

2:00–3:00 P.M.

_____

_____

3:00–4:00 P.M.

_____

_____

4:00–5:00 P.M.

_____

_____

5:00–6:00 P.M.

_____

_____

6:00–7:00 P.M.

_____

_____

7:00–8:00 P.M.

_____

_____

8:00–9:00 P.M.

_____

_____

9:00–10:00 P.M.

_____

_____

10:00 P.M.

_____

_____

Brainstorming

Circumstances often come up in life that need and demand our attention. Figuring out what to do about them may be difficult. Your own ideas for finding solutions may be limited by your experience or your involvement in the situation. But without a solution, a problem can cause your symptoms or circumstances to worsen. Brainstorming may help. Brainstorming can be used as a technique to address circumstances in your WRAP. Brainstorming is most effective in finding an appropriate response to triggers and early warning signs. When things are breaking down or you are in a crisis situation, this process can be very difficult. At these times, you will probably be better off following your predetermined plans.

Brainstorming refers to the process of jotting down, without thinking or editing, a variety of different options that *might* provide a solution to a difficult situation. You can do this alone or with others, but in order to get a diversity of ideas, it's best to do it with others. As you think of ideas and others share ideas, don't think up reasons why the idea wouldn't work. Just write it down. If the idea seems totally ludicrous, write it down anyway.

For instance, Susan was feeling tired all the time. She did a brainstorming session with her family (her partner, adult son, adult daughter, and her mother). She began by describing to them how she had been feeling. Then she asked for their ideas on possible actions she could take to reduce her fatigue and feel more energized. Their list included:

❑ beginning a program of daily exercise

❑ scheduling a physical examination

❑ asking family members to help with household chores

❑ working with a counselor on letting go of workaholic tendencies

❑ eliminating junk food from her diet

❑ working to lose ten pounds

❑ taking a multivitamin supplement

❑ taking the amino acids suggested by her naturopath

❑ clarifying her priorities and acting accordingly

❑ asking someone to watch her younger children on a regular basis

❑ going to bed by 10:30 A.M. every night

❑ getting a new mattress for the bed

❑ taking the train instead of driving to work

❑ discussing with her employer the possibility of working fewer hours

Then Susan reviewed the list alone, this time thinking carefully about each suggestion. Some of the actions were things she needed to do right away, like have a physical examination and discuss with her employer the possibility of working fewer hours. Other actions that felt right to her, like going to bed by 10:30 every night, taking a multivitamin supplement, beginning an exercise program, and asking someone to watch the children on a regular basis, could be part of her

WRAP. Other suggestions, like taking the train instead of driving to work (children's school schedules wouldn't allow this) and getting a new mattress for the bed (current financial limitations), weren't feasible at that time.

Try "brainstorming" by using the following guide. A duplicate of this form can be found in the appendix.

Situation or circumstance that needs to be addressed

_____

_____

Will you do the brainstorming exercise alone y _____ n _____ ? If no, who will you do the exercise with?

_____ /_____ /_____ /_____

_____ /_____ /_____ /_____

Ideas and suggestions

_____

_____

_____

_____

_____

_____

Of the ideas, which are actions that would be helpful to take right away?

_____

_____

_____

_____

Which are actions that you can include in your WRAP?

_____

_____

_____

_____

Which are actions that are not feasible to take at this time?

_____

_____

_____

_____

Diversionary and Creative Activities

Everyone has special activities that they really enjoy. They may be creative, educational, recreational, social, or just enjoyable. Like many others, you may find that you don't have time for these activities in the midst of your hectic life. Making time for these activities improves the quality of your life and can relieve uncomfortable feelings and stress.

These activities are very relaxing and can help reduce symptoms. They are an important part of any plan for responding to symptoms and creating life change. For example, Gary found himself overwhelmed with his busy life. He was trying to earn enough money through his vocation—tuning pianos—to provide care and support for his aging parents and to send his oldest child to college. He had a hard time turning down work and often worked ten to fifteen hours a day. When he was diagnosed with heart disease, he knew he had to slow down and take better care of himself. He realized it was many years since he had played his guitar, taken the time to read a book, or gone out to a movie. He was no longer taking the time to hike with friends or even go to work out at the health club. He began setting aside time and incorporating these activities back into his life. He knew the extra money that he would earn working overtime was not worth compromising his health.

Another example is that of Betty, who began climbing the corporate ladder after her children left home and her marriage ended. Working hard and not taking time for herself was a familiar path for her to take. She couldn't remember when she had painted a picture or taken part in a theatrical production—both of which had been consuming activities in her early adulthood.

Increased feelings of anxiety and an occasional panic attack, brought on because she was not taking time to do the things she needed to do to make herself feel good, convinced her that she needed to make some changes in her life. She enrolled in an evening painting class as a first step. She made a pact with herself to get out her paints every day, even if it was only for twenty minutes or half an hour. After she had firmly established this routine, she tried out for a small part in a local theatrical production. She got the part and went on to become more and more involved. As she integrated these activities into her life, her feelings of anxiety and panic attacks became a thing of the past.

What are some things that you really enjoy doing—the kind of things you really get "lost" in and that increase your feelings of well-being during and after the activity? The following examples may help you recall some activities you enjoy or have enjoyed in the past that can be part of your WRAP:

- ❏ woodworking
- ❏ sewing
- ❏ embroidery
- ❏ photography
- ❏ sculpting
- ❏ pottery
- ❏ fishing
- ❏ playing a musical instrument
- ❏ building musical instruments
- ❏ playing with a pet
- ❏ oil painting
- ❏ water colors
- ❏ charcoal drawings
- ❏ going to the movies
- ❏ walking
- ❏ playing cards
- ❏ basketball
- ❏ skiing
- ❏ gardening
- ❏ writing (poetry, fiction, nonfiction, plays, etc.)
- ❏ bird watching
- ❏ taking a college course in a subject that you find interesting
- ❏ surfing the internet

- ❏ knitting
- ❏ building models
- ❏ cooking
- ❏ metal work
- ❏ clay work
- ❏ ceramics
- ❏ fixing cars or other vehicles
- ❏ taking music lessons
- ❏ cooking
- ❏ quilting
- ❏ working with acrylics
- ❏ coloring
- ❏ carving
- ❏ dancing
- ❏ hiking
- ❏ soccer
- ❏ tennis
- ❏ snow boarding
- ❏ home maintenance activities
- ❏ reading fiction, comics, mystery novels, spiritual writings
- ❏ environmental study
- ❏ learning a new skill

Other creative or diversionary activities that you want to include in your WRAP:

_____

_____

_____

_____

Keep the materials and/or equipment you need for these activities in convenient places so you don't have to look for them when you need them. Remember, you are doing this to help yourself feel better and let out feelings and emotions. It is not to benefit someone else. It is not work to be judged or graded.

Often the hardest thing about integrating these activities into your life is getting started. Make a commitment to try an activity several times. If you enjoy it, make it part of your daily or weekly schedule. If you don't enjoy that one, try another. Keep working at it until you've discovered several creative activities you enjoy. For optimum wellness, spend some time every day doing one or more of these activities. You may want to spend a whole day or several days involved in these kinds of activities.

Journal Writing

People have kept diaries and written accounts of activities, events, dreams, thoughts, and feelings since the beginning of the written word. Recently, people have begun to fully recognize the power of this tool in dealing with various kinds of distress. Many people do it regularly no matter how they feel. Others write in their journal when they are having a difficult time. Writing for fifteen to thirty minutes a day can really help you enhance your awareness of your feelings, and journal writing is a great stress reliever.

Cheryl Coplan is a college professor who teaches journal writing courses in a community college and to groups of people in adult education programs. She says:

> There are many ways to use a journal in self-care. You can keep lists, record dreams, respond to questions, and explore your feelings. All ways are correct. Some of you may think that you won't be able to keep a journal because you don't write well enough. Please know that you keep a journal *just for you* and that you do just fine. It doesn't matter whether you use a bound, spiral, or loose-leaf notebook for your writing. It doesn't matter whether you use ruled or unruled paper.

Some suggestions for an optimal journal writing experience are: pick the type of paper that works for you; write with a pen that you feel comfortable with (many people like pens that allow them to write quickly and smoothly); keep your hand moving during the entire writing period; and keep your journal in a safe, private place.

Set the timer or put on your favorite music and begin to write. Do not edit your work or worry about spelling, just get your thoughts and feelings on paper. You may want to treat yourself to a fancy journal, or you may prefer to use an inexpensive spiral-bound notebook. Use whatever feels best to you.

During the allotted amount of time, write anything you want, anything you feel. It doesn't have to make sense. It doesn't have to be real. It doesn't need to be interesting. It's all right to repeat yourself over and over. Whatever is written is for you only. It's yours. Keep you hand moving. Try not to stop and think, just write whatever comes to mind. Avoid censoring or judging yourself or your writing. You don't have to worry about punctuation, grammar, spelling, penmanship, neatness, or staying on the lines. You can scribble all over the page if that makes you feel better. Don't fix your mistakes. Just keep writing. Doodle.

Anything goes. Some people like to draw or paste pictures or words in their journals.

Most people choose to keep their journal writings strictly confidential. The privacy of the journal should not be violated by anyone. You don't have to share your writings with anybody unless you want to. You may want to put a note in the front of your journal that says something like, "This contains private information. Please do not read it without my permission. Thank you." Some people find it helpful and feel comfortable sharing writings with family members, friends, or health care professionals. This is a personal choice.

It helps to set aside a time every day for journaling. It may be early in the morning or before going to sleep at night. Spend as little or as much time writing as you want. Some people like to set a timer. You can write in your journal anytime—daily, several times a day, weekly, before you go to bed, when you wake up, after supper, whenever you feel like it—the choice is yours. You don't have to commit to keeping a journal for the rest of your life—just use it when you feel like it or you think it would be helpful in enhancing your wellness.

Bill, who is dealing with a chronic pain condition, uses journal writing as part of his WRAP. When his pain worsens, the tension in his body increases. The tension seems to exacerbate the pain. When he realizes that's happening, he gets out his journal and writes. Often it's just scribbling. But as he writes, the tension drains out of him and the pain seems to decrease.

If you have a hard time getting started, try responding to some of the following questions:

- ❏ If your life could be any way you wanted, what would it be like?

- ❏ What do you like about yourself?

- ❏ What is making you feel good today?

- ❏ What made you feel sad today?

- ❏ What made you feel happy and excited today?

- ❏ What are the stresses in your life? What can you do about them?

- ❏ What makes you happy?

- ❏ Who are your favorite people?

- ❏ Write a letter to someone you would like to "tell off," but you know it wouldn't be wise, or to someone who is not available (i.e., you're no longer in contact, they are deceased).

- ❏ Write a letter to yourself when you were a small child.

- ❏ Write a letter to yourself, pretending you are your own best friend.

- ❏ List the best things that have happened this day (month, year) in your life.

- ❏ Finish the sentence: The best thing that ever happened to me was . . .

- ❏ Finish the sentence: The worst thing that ever happened to me was . . .

- ❏ Finish the sentence: I want to be alive because . . .

List other questions or topics you could write about in your journal:

_____

_____

_____

_____

Use Your Spiritual Resources

Many people report that they find it very helpful to reach out for spiritual support on a regular basis, as well as whenever they are having a hard time. Spiritual resources and making use of those resources varies from person to person. For some people it means to pray, go to church, or reach out to a member of the clergy. For others it is meditation, affirmations, and other kinds of inspirational readings. It may include rituals and ceremonial services.

For example, Mary, who is Roman Catholic, has had recurring bouts of breast cancer. She has found that weekly church attendance helps her maintain her wellness and reduces her anxiety about her illness. When she has early warning signs that the cancer is recurring, she finds that going to mass daily helps relieve her anxiety and deal with day-to-day issues in a more positive way.

Do Something Normal

When you don't feel "like yourself" or feel "normal," it helps to do something normal—the kind of thing you do every day or at least frequently—things that are part of your routine, such as:

❏ shaving

❏ washing your hair

❏ calling a friend or family member

❏ walking the dog

❏ taking a shower

❏ making yourself a sandwich

❏ making your bed

❏ getting gas in the car

When you are having a hard time, you may feel like everything in your life is "out of synch." This increases anxiety and gets in the way of relaxation and wellness. Doing things that you always do can reduce this anxiety. For instance, when Claire's psoriasis (a skin condition) is worsening, she feels like her life is "topsy turvy." She has noticed that doing her daily chores, like washing the dishes and making the beds, helps her to feel better and even reduces her awareness of the itching.

The next chapter is designed to help you set up a support system. While it is important to be responsible for your WRAP and take action for your own wellness, having family members, friends, and health care providers lend support is a crucial part of WRAP.

Chapter 6

Setting Up a Support System and Self-Advocating

You and Your Health Care Providers

As you begin setting up or expanding your support system, it is important that you include your health care providers. In order to best incorporate them into your support system, you (or someone you love if you are unable to do so) must work closely with your health care providers, asking questions and providing them with as much information as possible. Following are some suggestions and reminders for getting the most out of your health care.

Get a Physical Examination

There may be a point where a physical examination is necessary. It may be when:

- your symptoms change significantly or worsen

- you feel like you are not making any progress toward wellness

- it is necessitated by testing needs, such as when you are using certain medications

- you have not had a physical in the past year

To insure that you get the best possible physical examination, you can assist the physician in his or her detective work by filling in the following form before going to see the doctor. Fill it out several days in advance of your visit, giving yourself space to think of any additional information that needs to be added. Make an extra copy so you have one for yourself. Give it to the doctor to review at the beginning of your examination. Review it again at the end of your visit to insure that all important issues have been addressed to your satisfaction. The following form is duplicated in the appendix.

Information for the Physician

1. All medications, vitamins, and health care preparations you are using for any reason.

Medication	Dosage	When	How Used

2. A medical history of yourself and your family.

Your history

Your Mother's Side of the Family

Your Father's Side of the Family

3. Describe changes in the following aspects of your health.

Your appetite or diet: _____

_____

Your weight: _____

_____

Your sleep patterns: _____

_____

Your sexual interest: _____

_____

Your ability to concentrate: _____

_____

Your memory: _____

_____

Have you recently had:

❏   headaches (describe) _____

❏   numbness or tingling anywhere (where) _____

❏   loss of balance (describe) _____

❏   double vision or vision problems (describe) _____

❏   periods of amnesia (describe) _____

❏   coordination changes (describe) _____

❏   weakness in arms or legs (describe) _____

❏   fever (describe) _____

❏   nausea or diarrhea (describe) _____

❏   other gastrointestinal problems (describe) _____

❏   fainting or dizziness (describe) _____

❏   seizures (describe) _____

❏   stressful life events (describe) _____

Add additional sheets for other pertinent information.

Other Things to Keep in Mind:

• If you are taking medication, new symptoms or an exacerbation of symptoms warrants a medication check with the prescribing physician.

• Whenever things aren't going well or aren't going as well as expected, it's a good idea to get together with your health care professionals to discuss a change in your treatment. It's best if all of the health care professionals who provide you with care get together and work with you to come up with a treatment plan.

• When you are receiving treatment, you have the right to a second opinion. Many people feel that asking for a second opinion will "hurt the feelings" of their health care professional. A good health care professional is not concerned when you take advantage of that option. The value of your treatment may be limited if you have concerns about whether or not it is the right treatment for you or if you have concerns about its safety. If the recommendations of two health care professionals are not in agreement, you should probably search out a third opinion.

• If you are not satisfied with the answers provided by your doctor, or you and/or your doctor feel your needs could be better addressed by someone else, particularly someone who specializes in an area of concern to you, ask your doctor for a referral. You may have to use your assertiveness skills to get this referral (either with your doctor or your health insurance carrier), but don't give up until you get care and treatment that feels right to you.

• Ask your health care provider if hot or cold packs would help an injured part of your body or would help you to feel better.

• There are many therapies that may assist you in attaining the highest levels of physical wellness. Some, such as physical and occupational therapy, are covered by many insurance and health care plans. Others, like dance, movement, or art therapy may not be covered by your insurance, but, if you can afford them, they may be helpful in reducing your physical and/or emotional symptoms.

• There are many competent massage therapists available who can give you a relaxing and rejuvenating massage. They have been trained to work with people with a variety of health problems and life issues. They often use a variety of techniques, which they can describe to you. You can ask them for the kind of massage that feels right to you. Ask your friends for referrals to a good massage therapist.

• You don't need any special training to gently rub parts of your own body. Avoid doing anything that feels painful. A foot massage is especially easy to do on your own.

• Acupuncture is a Chinese practice that includes painless insertion of very thin needles into the surface of the skin. Its use by alternative and mainstream health care practitioners is increasing. Many people find it to be helpful in relieving all kinds of symptoms. If this sounds like something you would like to try, ask your friends and health care providers for referrals.

- Acupressure is similar to acupuncture, except that rather than using needles, gentle pressure is applied at various points on the body.

- There may be some vitamins, minerals, herbs, amino acids, and other food supplements that will reduce your symptoms and enhance an overall sense of well-being. The optimum way to find out which of these products would be helpful and safe for you to use is through consultation with a health care professional, such as a naturopathic physician, who has extensive training and experience in their use. However, the cost of such a consultation may be prohibitive for you. Some health care plans are now providing coverage for these services, but this is the exception rather than the rule. Only by letting our elected officials know that these services should be covered, and that they often prevent more costly health care, will this picture change.

- There are many excellent reference books and resources available that can help you decide which health care products would be good options for you. Most health food stores have an extensive section of literature that can provide you with the guidance you need. Check out the qualifications of the authors before making decisions. Store personnel are also a source of useful information. If you are going to try food supplements, never use more than the recommended dosages, carefully monitor how you are feeling when you are using these supplements, and discontinue their use if you notice unusual side effects.

Obtaining Assistance and Support

Asking others for help and support is often very difficult. However, there are times when both assistance and support are very important, even essential. Many people, especially those who have been sick for a long time or who have emotional problems, may not have a strong group of people who can support them or provide them with assistance. In this case, your WRAP may begin with developing a support system.

Developing a Strong Support System

Often, one of the most effective responses to symptoms is reaching out to a very good friend, family member, or health care professional, and either telling them how you are feeling or just spending time with them doing something you both enjoy. Everyone needs and deserves at least several friends or supporters who:

- listen to you

- have interests similar to yours

- respect your need for confidentiality

- you can have a good time with

- you like, respect, and trust, and who like, respect, and trust you

- support you in sharing anything you feel comfortable with

- let you freely express your feelings and emotions without judging or criticizing

- give you good advice when you want and ask for it

- allow you the space to change, grow, make decisions, and even mistakes

- accept your good and bad moods

- work with you to figure out what to do next in difficult situations

- assist you in taking action that will help you feel better

- make you feel good about yourself when you are with them

If you have at least five friends or supporters who you feel meet your needs in these ways, you are very fortunate. You can never have too many friends like this, so you may choose to continue building such friendships. If you find that you have fewer than five people whom you consider close supporters, or if you feel that there is no one you can turn to when you are having a hard time, you may need to work on developing a support team. It's not hopeless. You *can* take action to change the situation.

Making friends is a skill like other skills—it can be learned. You may have trouble making friends and developing supporters for a lot of different reasons. One of these reasons may be that you don't feel good about yourself, so you can't imagine that anyone would like you. If you don't feel good about yourself and it keeps you from having friends and supporters, get a good book on raising self-esteem (see Resources section for suggestions of books on this topic) and work on it until you feel better about yourself. For now, keep in mind that even if you don't like yourself, it doesn't mean someone else won't.

Another potential reason you're having difficulty building and maintaining friendships could be that you expect your friends to be perfect, so you can't find anyone who meets your standards. If this is true for you, work on changing these negative standards to: "No one is perfect, but there are many wonderful people who would like to be my friend and supporter."

Or perhaps you are shy and don't know how to reach out to others. Practice being comfortable with others by joining a school club, church group, or community group. It's always hard to go the first time. You may feel as if you will stand out like a "sore thumb." Ignore those feelings, and go to activities that interest you. When you have talked to the same person at several activities, ask that person to join you in an activity of mutual interest. That's how friendships develop.

Another possibility is that you may be sensitive to any sign of potential rejection and react to it by giving up on the other person. Avoid giving up on people until you are absolutely sure they can't be supportive. Talk to others about what you are feeling, and encourage them to share how they are feeling. Work together so you can both feel good in the relationship.

Perhaps you haven't had the opportunity to develop the social skills necessary to make and keep friends and supporters. If you feel this may be the case, discuss it with someone you trust. Tell this person that you have a hard time getting and keeping friends and supporters, and ask them if there is something you are doing that is turning off others. Be prepared for them to give you an honest answer. Once you know what the problem is, you can work on correcting it.

The following attitudes and behaviors tend to "turn off" others and hamper the development of friendships:

- being overly dependent or needy

- expecting too much

- lack of attention to the needs of others

- blaming and "bad mouthing" others

- gossip and rumor spreading

- negativity

- constant chatter

- expecting the other person to carry all of the conversation

- inattentiveness when others are talking

- invalidating the feelings of others

- lack of attention to personal hygiene

- excessive foul language

- lying

Another possible explanation is that you don't have ongoing contact with others who might become friends and supporters. Join a support, community, church, or special-interest group. Attend activities you think you might enjoy.

When you feel you have developed a special rapport with another person that feels like real friendship (i.e., the person seems as interested and as eager to spend time with you as you are to spend time with them), make a plan to get together. The first time you meet could be a low-key activity, such as eating lunch together or taking a walk.

Don't overwhelm the person with phone calls. Use your intuition and common sense to determine when to call and how often. Don't ever call late at night or early in the morning until you both have agreed to be available to each other in case of emergency. As you feel more and more comfortable with the other person, you will likely find that you talk more and share more personal information. Make sure you have a mutual understanding that anything the two of you discuss that is personal is absolutely confidential, and *never* make fun of what the other person thinks or feels. Avoid judging or criticizing the other person.

Each time you get together with new friends, try to end that time by making a plan for the next time you will be together. If something comes up you want to share in the meantime, you can arrange a get-together by phone or in person, but always having something planned can reinforce the strength of the friendship.

Following are some ways you can meet people with whom you might develop supportive relationships:

- Attending a support group. Support groups are a great way to make new friends. It could be a group for people who have similar health issues or challenges, similar life challenges, or a group for people of a particular sex or age.

- Go to community events. Let yourself be seen and known in the communities you want to be a part of on a regular basis.

- Join a special-interest club. These are often listed in the newspaper. In these groups, you will meet people with whom you already share a common interest. It might be a group that is focused on hiking, bird watching, stamp collecting, cooking, music, literature, sports, or any number of other interests.

- Take a course. Adult education programs, community colleges, and universities offer courses that will facilitate meeting new people. Another benefit is that you will learn something interesting that might even open the doors to a new career or a career change.

- Volunteer. Offer to assist a school, hospital, or organization in your community.

Using Your Support System

It is important that when you need support, you let the supporter know what you want and need. For instance, you may say, "Today I need you to just listen to me." Following are some other suggestions that will enable you to use and maintain your support system:

- Spend as much time listening and paying attention to your friends and supporters as they spend paying attention and listening to you, unless you are feeling physically or psychologically unable to do so. Whenever you are unable to be mutually supportive to friends and family members, be sure you pay attention to them another time.

- Spend most of your time with supporters doing fun, interesting activities together. This will prevent them from feeling like they are burdened or that you are just spending time with them to receive their support.

- Take turns suggesting and initiating activities.

- Keep regular contact with your friends, even when things are going well.

- Do everything you can to keep yourself well and stable. Make your wellness your highest priority. Stick with your daily maintenance plan. Others don't have a lot of patience with people who don't take good care of themselves. If you consistently miss health care appointments, neglect healthy lifestyle habits, and sabotage your efforts to keep yourself well, friends and supporters may back away.

- Work on changing any bad habits you have identified that keep people from wanting to be your friends or supporters.

- Be mutually supportive. Be there for others when they need you, and ask them to be there for you when you need them.

- Try peer or exchange counseling with your friends or supporters. (More information on how to do this is provided later in this chapter.)

- Have a goal of having at least five good friends or supporters. Make a list of your support team members with their phone numbers. When you most need to reach out, it can be the hardest to remember who your friends and supporters are, or to find their phone numbers. Have copies of the list of your supporters by your phone and in your wallet.

Post the following list on your bulletin board or refrigerator door and in the front of your WRAP binder (a duplicate of this form is available in the appendix):

Support List

Name	Phone Number	Activities to Share

Peer Counseling

Peer counseling is a structured way of getting the attention and support you need when difficult symptoms come up or when you are trying to cope with the stress of daily living. It can help you express your feelings, understand your problems, discover some helpful action you can take, and even feel better. When used consistently, it is a free, safe, and effective self-help tool that encourages expression of feelings and emotions and promotes wellness.

Peer counseling also provides you with an opportunity to give support to someone else. Both aspects of peer counseling help relieve symptoms: being heard, allowing you to address your feelings and issues, and listening, giving you an opportunity to support someone else. Peer counseling is an opportunity to express yourself any way you choose, while supported by a trusted friend and ally.

When difficult symptoms and situations are present in your life, you may find yourself going over and over the same problem or problems in your mind. You may feel unable to come to any resolution about how to address the situation, or you may be unable to let go of the circumstance and get on with something else. The process of sharing the situation with an attentive listener helps give perspective and organize your thoughts. At the end of a session, you may find that you have determined a new or better course of action, or you may feel ready to let go of obsessing about the situation.

Peer counseling is not the same as working with a professional counselor, therapist, or mental health worker. A counselor or therapist has special skills and experience that they use to provide you with assistance in dealing with issues in your life. A peer counselor provides listening only and does not give advice. Peer counseling is not the same as a conversation. In a conversation, two or more people get together to discuss issues and experiences of mutual interest. There is no attempt made to insure equal time, and in conversation there is a give and take that is not part of peer counseling.

In a peer counseling session, two people who like and trust each other agree to spend a previously agreed upon amount of time together, dividing the time equally, addressing and paying attention to each other's issues. For instance, if you have decided you will spend an hour together, the first half hour is focused on one person and the second half hour on the other person. Sessions can be as short or as long as the two participants would like them to be. Often the length of time is predetermined by the demands of busy lives and hectic schedules. I have done peer counseling for ten minutes—with each person getting five minutes to talk and five minutes to listen—and for three hours—with each person getting ninety minutes to talk and ninety minutes to listen. Each was powerful and effective in its own way.

It should be understood by both you and the other participant that the content of these sessions is strictly confidential. Information that a person shares in a session is never shared with anyone. If there is a possibility that either of the participants might share information that would lead the listener to believe that the person who is talking is a danger to themselves or others, there should be a prior agreement on how such a situation would be handled. Most people agree that confidentiality must be violated if there is a possibility that a participant is a danger to themselves or someone else.

Judging, criticizing, and giving advice are not allowed. When the person is having their time to be heard, the listener should only make an occasional neutral comment to the person who is talking like "I understand," "I'm sorry you are having such a hard time," or "I'm here for you."

Sessions should be held in a comfortable, quiet place where there will be no interruption or distraction, and where the session cannot be heard by others. Disconnect the phone, turn off the radio and television, find someone to watch small children, and do whatever else is necessary to eliminate distractions. While most people prefer sessions where they meet in person, they can be held over the phone when necessary.

The content of the session is determined by the person who is being heard and is receiving attention—the "talker." The talker can use their time any way they choose. It may include eager talk, reluctant talk, tears, crying, trembling, ranting, indignant storming, laughter, yawning, shaking, singing, or punching a pillow. You may want to spend some time planning your life and goals. The only thing that is not okay is for the talker to hurt the listener or themselves.

As the talker, you may find it useful to focus on one issue and keep coming back to it despite feelings of wanting to avoid it. At other times, you may find yourself switching from subject to subject. At the beginning of a session, you may want to focus on one particular issue, but as you proceed, you may find other issues coming up that take precedence. All of this is up to you. The person who is listening and paying attention needs to do only that—be an attentive, supportive listener.

It is especially important to remember that in peer counseling, the expression of emotion is *never* seen as a symptom of a psychiatric illness. Emotion is not so much a sign that something is wrong with you as it is a vital part of the wellness process. Repressing emotion interferes with your wellness.

This was a hard thing for Bill to believe, as he was taught not to cry or openly express emotions when he was young. When he cried, he was called a cry baby and reminded that "men" don't cry. Occasionally he was even punished or sent to his room for crying. As an adult, he felt stifled in his ability to express emotions. He felt it was aggravating his ongoing problem with episodes of depression and anxiety. On the advice of a friend, he decided to give peer counseling a try. At first, he couldn't express any emotion. But as he got more comfortable with his peer counseling partner, and observed his partner expressing emotion in a healthy and positive way, he became more comfortable with expressing emotion. He often cried or visibly trembled as he shared the circumstances of his life. As his ability to express his emotions increased, he noticed a decrease in the severity of both the depression and anxiety.

The following techniques will help you increase the effectiveness of peer counseling:

- The talker can make requests of the listener that assist in the process of releasing emotions or enhancing understanding such as: "Tell me what you like about me," or "Pretend you are my _____ (parent, friend, employer, etc.) so I can safely practice telling her/him how I feel or what I want."

- You may notice that when you are peer counseling, you say the same negative things about yourself over and over again. This is not helpful and could even worsen depression or other symptoms. When you realize you are doing this, you can change the negative statements to positive ones and repeat these statements over and over again in the peer counseling session. Before long, you will know that these positive statements are true and you will eventually feel better, even though at first it may make you feel worse. When people begin saying these positive statements over and over to themselves, they often find themselves crying or releasing emotions in some way.

  For example, when Andrew first began peer counseling, he would repeat over and over, "I never do anything right." He changed that negative thought to, "I do lots of things well," and repeated that over and over. When he first said "I do lots of things well," feelings of sadness filled him and his eyes filled with tears. The more he said it over time, however, the better he felt and the more he believed the positive thought.

- When your symptoms are making you feel uncomfortable and keeping you from doing the things you need to do and the things you enjoy doing, it may be most helpful to focus peer counseling sessions on getting things back in order in your life and focusing your attention away from past issues. Sometimes it helps to focus your peer counseling session on the present, putting your attention on pleasant things and your life as it is now. Do whatever feels best to you.

• Keep the peer counseling session contained so that the session will leave the talkers in a more positive place than they were in when they started. This will help ensure that the time when you are not peer counseling can be used to do things you enjoy and to manage your life. The session can be kept contained using the following methods: First, at the beginning of a session, the listener can ask the talker to share several good things that have happened in the last week (or day, or month). This provides a positive starting point for the session. Then, at the end of the session, the listener can ask the talker to share something they are looking forward to doing in the next week.

The value of peer counseling is being recognized by more and more people who are working to improve their levels of wellness and the overall quality of their lives.

Asking People to Help You

You may have a hard time asking for things. Try to get in the habit of asking others for help when you need it. Note in your plan when you need to ask others for help, what kind of help you may need, and who to ask. When you are having a hard time, people often wonder what they can do to help. Help them out by asking them directly for whatever it is you need.

Receiving Professional Help

Professional Counseling

If you are working with a counselor, you may want to include calling your counselor or scheduling additional time with your counselor under specific circumstances. You may want to talk with your counselor about this possibility. Let her or him know under what circumstances you would want to be in touch.

Calling Warm and Hot Lines

Many communities have phone lines available that provide information and support. Some are general (i.e., they address any kind of problem or issue) while others deal with specific issues (i.e., AIDS, depression and suicide, or parenting). A warm line provides a free phone connection with a supportive person. People who answer the phones are usually trained to listen, provide feedback, provide encouragement, and be supportive. Many of them have specific hours when they are available. Post phone numbers of warm lines that you include in your plan in convenient places.

Hot line workers are trained to provide the same services as a warm line. In addition, they can provide referrals. If they feel you are in a crisis, or are a danger to yourself or others, they will arrange for immediate help. These numbers are listed in the front of the phone book.

Bringing Your Support System Together

Plan some activity that will allow the friends and family members in your support group to meet each other and get support for yourself. One way to do this is to host a potluck meal. All you have to do is invite people with a simple phone call, and provide the space, dishes, and silverware. Each person brings whatever they want. You might want to ask people to choose a category such as main dish, salad, vegetable, bread, dessert, or beverage to avoid getting all the same kinds of food, but sometimes it's fun to just have people bring whatever they want and see what happens. You can have a potluck for as few as three people—one person brings the main dish, another a salad, and the third brings a bread. You could provide the beverage and a simple dessert. The dessert is really optional. Fresh fruit or fresh fruit and cheese is easy and most people enjoy it. You could choose an activity such as a game or a walk after the meal if that feels right to you.

You may also wish to have a more formal meeting of your supporters or your family. Invite them and tell them what you want and need from them as you are trying to take positive action to create change in your life. Ask them to be honest with you about what they are willing or not willing to do. Share your plans with them if you feel comfortable doing this.

In the next chapter, you will work on increasing positive feelings about yourself. Self-esteem is a crucial element to your wellness.

Chapter 7

Increasing Your
Self-Esteem

Making Yourself Feel Good

Low self-esteem seems to exist in epidemic proportions throughout our society. If you have any negative perceptions of yourself, it has an impact on every aspect of your life. It doesn't matter where you got them—messages from peers, siblings, friends, school, church, the media, parents or other adults (when you were a child)—raising your self-esteem will improve the quality of your life. In your WRAP, you may want to work on raising your self-esteem. In the first part of this chapter, I will discuss several things you can do to combat negative self-image or low self-esteem. You may also want to think of other ways to raise your self-esteem as you work on developing your plans. There are also entire books devoted to this topic that you may want to read if you continue to struggle with low self-esteem (see Resources).

Surround Yourself with People Who Are Positive, Affirming, and Loving

Sometimes you may forget that you have control over the people with whom you spend time. Think about how the people in your life make you feel about yourself. If you don't feel good when you are around them, spend less time with them. Spend more time with people who do make you feel good. Avoid people who abuse you in any way.

Wear Something That Makes You Feel Good

Everybody has certain clothes or jewelry that they enjoy wearing because they make you feel comfortable and/or attractive. These are the things to wear when you are having a hard time, when your symptoms are more severe, when you have to keep a dreaded appointment, or when you have to have an uncomfortable treatment or procedure. If you don't have a supply of clothes that make you feel good or that fit well, buy yourself some. If your financial resources are limited, check out thrift stores. They often have very good buys. If you can't go shopping yourself, ask a trusted friend to do this for you with the understanding that you can return those clothes that you don't like or that don't fit.

Look Through Old Pictures, Scrapbooks, and Photo Albums

Many of us neglect to look at reminders of our past that make us feel good. An hour or two involved in this pleasurable activity could help you feel a lot better. If you'd like to spend an extended amount of time doing this, you can engage in activities such as organizing your photos into annotated scrapbooks or making a collage of your life. Let the child inside of you come out and play. Get a supply of old colorful magazines, scissors, glue, markers, glitter, heavy paper, and anything else that you can think of that would enhance the project. Then create a colorful celebration of you, your life, an event, a series of events, or a major accomplishment. Cut, paste, and draw until you have a creation you feel good about.

Reminding Yourself of Your Positive Achievements and Attributes

Try making a list of your accomplishments. Get a big sheet of paper and a pen you feel comfortable with. Set the timer for twenty minutes (or as long as you'd like). Write as many of your accomplishments as you can in the allotted amount of time. This list can include things like:

- learning to talk
- learning to read
- making a good friend
- taking care of a younger sibling
- making the bed
- getting a job
- keeping a houseplant alive for a year

- learning to walk
- climbing a tree
- keeping a good friend
- reading a good book
- taking a shower
- doing the dishes
- getting a C in algebra (for some people, just sitting through the course is an accomplishment)

Another exercise along these lines is spending ten minutes writing down everything good you can think of about yourself. Begin with a piece of paper you like and a pen that feels good to you. Set a timer if you have one. If not, just keep track of the time. Write down all the good things you can think of about yourself. If you can't think of different things, write the same things over and over again. Don't worry about spelling or grammar. When you are finished, reread it. Then put it in a safe place. Read it again before you go to bed at night, after you get up in the morning, and any time you have free time during the day. Read it to yourself or read it aloud. Read it to someone who loves you.

Do Things That Make You Laugh

What makes you laugh? Are there certain comedians, jokes, movies, or videos, or people you know? The old television show *Candid Camera* helped its host, Norman Cousins, laugh his way out of a terrible illness. Use your ingenuity to put things that make you laugh within easy reach when you need them—things like copies of television shows, comic books, and videos.

Do Something Special for Someone Else

Have you ever noticed the good feeling that "washes over you" when you do something nice for someone else? If so, take advantage of that good feeling to keep yourself feeling well. You can do this when you are having a hard time or any time you see an opportunity or can fit it in. This could include:

- sending someone special a greeting card
- calling a friend to wish them well
- visiting someone who is unable to get out and socialize (i.e., nursing home residents, hospital patients, or shut-ins)
- playing a game with a child
- reading stories to a group of children
- pushing a child on the swing at a park
- taking someone who is having a hard time to the movies
- baking or cooking for a family member
- raking your neighbor's leaves

Pretend You Are Your Own Best Friend

This is a technique that I have often used. When I make decisions about taking care of myself, my priorities may not be in my best interest. I find it helpful to decide what to do based on what I presume my best friend would tell me to do.

For example, I may decide that I am going to spend all evening writing a report for work instead of taking care of myself and doing things I enjoy. If I look at this situation as if I am my own best friend, I will change my mind, leaving the report until the next day.

Get Some Little Things Done

It always helps you feel better about yourself if you accomplish something, even if it is a very small thing. Think of some easy things to do that don't take much time. Then do them. Some ideas include:

- clean out one drawer
- dust a bookcase
- read a page in a favorite book
- do a load of laundry
- send someone a card
- put five pictures in a photo album
- hang a picture
- make the bed
- cook yourself something healthy
- weed one small section of your garden

Repeating Positive Affirmations

Affirmations, when repeated, can help you overcome negative thoughts or feelings about yourself. You can make you own affirmations, based on rebutting negative self-talk that you find yourself repeating to yourself. For example, if you often think, "No one likes me," "I'm no good," or "I don't deserve anything in life," repeat a positive affirmation like the following over and over to yourself: "I am a wonderful and very special person. I have many unique qualities. I deserve the best that life has to offer." While it may seem difficult or insincere at first, eventually the more positive thoughts will replace the negative ones.

Balance

Everyone has strengths and talents. However, you, like many people, may get stuck focusing on what you see as your weaknesses and faults. By working on achieving a sense of balance, you will recognize when you have gone to one extreme or the other—from seeing everything you do as either flawed or infallible. Achieving balance can help prevent you from letting one incident effect how you feel about yourself and using that incident in isolation to harshly judge yourself. As you bring yourself back to a more reasonable view of yourself, you will be a better judge of who you really are, and hopefully you can become accepting and encouraging of yourself.

Jane Winterling shares the following example that illustrates the importance of keeping a sense of balance:

> One day my fifteen-year-old daughter thought I was handling a situation with her sister wrong. She told me in no uncertain terms that I was wrong and that I was a terrible mother. I used this incident to reflect on my mothering for the past fifteen years, paying attention

to all the mistakes I had made. It felt awful. I then remembered a technique I had used to help myself. I visualized that when I got to Heaven's gate, St. Peter was there to do the judging, and when he opened his book he would say, "I see here on July 16, 1998, your daughter said you made a mistake and were a terrible mother. Well that does it! You are going to Hell!" Of course, I started to laugh. I started to remember all the good things I had done as a parent and felt better about myself. Then I proceeded to take the action in my daughter's behalf that I knew was right. I have learned it is important not to judge myself based on any one incident or any one person's feelings about me at a given moment.

Changing Thoughts and Feelings

As part of developing your plans, you may recognize the need to create changes in the way you think and feel. This process takes consistency and persistence. Your WRAP plans can help keep you on track.

One of the wonderful things research has discovered is that your mind is like the other parts of your body—it responds to exercise and training. With time and persistence, you can overcome bad habits and negative thought patterns. Following are some useful things to know about how the mind works:

- You can only think about one thing at a time. Try thinking about two things at one time simultaneously. You may be able to jump back and forth quickly, but you can't think of both of them at exactly the same moment.

- The mind is like the heart. It never stops.

- You can learn to control what you think. If your mind is going too fast, you can use one of the many relaxation and stress reduction exercises to slow your thinking down. If your mind gets stuck on a particularly upsetting topic, you can try exercises that include counting or focusing your thoughts on your breath, which can allow you to shift your focus.

- There is a mind/body connection. When your mind is upset, your body reacts by becoming upset as well. It also works the other way around. If your body is calm and quiet, your mind will slow down. If you know certain topics are upsetting to you, you may decide to avoid them in conversation, videos, television, radio, magazines, and the newspaper. Jane Winterling says:

  I went through a period of time when I was very self-conscious about my weight. I realized I was becoming obsessive about it—basing my self-esteem on a half pound weight gain or loss. At that time I was also reading a lot of women's magazines. I think there is at least one article on weight loss in every women's magazine. Since I stopped reading these magazines, I have found I spend much less time thinking about weight and a lot more time thinking about things that are important to me. I also have found that if some of these thought patterns creep back in, my efforts to counteract them are much more effective.

Changing Negative Thoughts, Attitudes, and Beliefs

When you are triggered or when symptoms start to appear, you may notice that you have negative thoughts, attitudes, and beliefs about yourself that worsen the situation. These may worsen as your symptoms worsen. For instance, Sylvia noticed that when she is triggered by receiving a bigger than expected bill in the mail, she immediately starts giving herself negative messages like: "I am a bad person because I don't make enough money," "I always spend too much money," "I never do anything right," and "I'll never make it." As she repeats these negative messages over and over to herself, she feels worse and worse. She has found that instead of responding to a trigger with negative self-talk, she can give herself positive messages like: "I do the best I can," "Everyone overspends sometimes," "I can pay this off a little bit at a time, and I won't really notice it," "There are lots of things I do very well," and "I have already made it. I have a good job and a wonderful circle of friends." When she repeats these positive messages to herself, over time she noticed that she began to feel better and better.

With persistence and time, you can change negatives thoughts, attitudes, and beliefs to positive ones, helping yourself to feel better. It takes hard work and persistence, as it does in overcoming any addictive behavior, but it's worth it. The following steps describe a process for changing negative thoughts to positive ones.

Step One: Identifying Your Negative Thoughts or Attitudes

The first step in this process is discovering your negative thoughts. They are often so much a part of you that this may be a difficult task. Get a small pad to carry with you and jot down any negative thoughts that you notice throughout the day. Be especially aware of negative thought patterns when you have been triggered. Ask a close friend or family member if they have noticed any negative thoughts or attitudes characteristic of you.

Some examples of common negative thoughts are:

- I never accomplish anything.

- I never do anything right.

- Everything I do always turns out badly.

- It seems as if they like me now, but I'm sure they will stop liking me when they find out what I'm really like.

- My partner will find someone else that he or she prefers to be with.

- I'm not attractive enough to have a relationship.

- I always say the wrong thing at the wrong time.

- I'll never be able to get this done.

- I'm not good at anything.

- I'll never be able to hold down a job.
- I'll never be able to get a job doing what I really want to be doing.
- My job will end when my employer finds out I'm not really competent.
- My partner didn't call me tonight. She or he must have found someone new.
- The teacher must think I'm stupid because she or he didn't call on me when I raised my hand.
- I don't look good without my makeup.
- The worst possible thing will happen every time.
- I am not as smart as my peers.
- If I feel like something bad is going to happen, something bad will happen.
- If only my partner would come home for dinner on time, everything would be great.
- No one will ever care about me.
- I should always dress up or people won't respect me.
- I have to do everything perfectly.

Often these kinds of worries are about future events and are not supported by present circumstances. Use the following space to list negative thoughts and/or attitudes that cause you worry or discomfort:

_____

_____

_____

_____

Step Two: Checking the Validity of Negative Thoughts

The process of analyzing your negative thoughts to see if they are really true is often helpful in taking the power from these thought patterns. Choose a negative thought from the list you developed in step one of this process (e.g., "I never do anything right") and use it to complete the following sheet (a blank copy is in the appendix).

Your negative thought _____

Ask yourself the following questions about the thought. Be honest with yourself. Skip over those questions which do not apply to your negative thoughts or attitudes.

1. Is this negative thought or attitude *really* true? (Give yourself the benefit of the doubt. Provide supporting evidence to the contrary.)
   [Sample answer in response to "I never do anything right": It's not really true. I do lots of things very well. They include: cooking, gardening, driving a car, and caring for my child.]

2. Would a person who really cares about you be thinking this about you? If not, then should you be saying it to yourself?
   [Sample response to "I never do anything right": No one who really cared about a person would ever think, "They can't do anything right." So I shouldn't be saying it to myself.]

3. Ask other people you trust: Do you think this negative thought or attitude is true?
   [Sample response to "I never do anything right": My friend said of course that wasn't true. She pointed out how successful I am at work and reminded me that she thought I was a good friend, and that being her friend was something that I had done really well.]

4. What do you get out of thinking your negative thought or attitude? How does it help? How does it hurt?
   [Sample response to "I never do anything right": I don't get anything out of saying to myself "I can't do anything right." It makes me feel terrible. It causes me to worry about things.]

Often this step of analyzing your negative thought is all that is needed to get rid of it. However, with most negative thoughts, you will need to do more work to get the negative thought out of your consciousness for good.

Step Three: Developing Positive Thoughts to Contradict Negative Ones

The next step is developing positive statements that contradict the negative messages you have been giving yourself. Working with the same negative thought you worked with above, write a positive thought that is the opposite of the negative thought.

[Sample response to "I never do anything right": I could say, "I do lots of things right."]

Write a positive statement that is the opposite of your negative thought.

_____

_____

Avoid using negative words in your positive thoughts such as *frightened, upset, tired, bored, not, never, can't.* Use only positive words like *happy, peaceful, loving, enthusiastic, warm,* and *can.* Substitute "it would be nice if" for "should."

Following are some examples of negative thoughts that may increase worry and some positive responses to counteract them:

Negative Thought: I will never feel good again.

Positive Response: I feel better and better each day.

Negative Thought: I am not worth anything.

Positive Response: I am a valuable person.

Negative Thought: It's not okay to make mistakes.

Positive Response: It's okay to make mistakes. Nobody's perfect.

Negative Thought: No one will ever like me.

Positive Response: Many people like me.

Negative Thought: I always make the wrong choice.

Positive Response: I make many good choices.

Negative Thought: I'm stupid.

Positive Response: I'm knowledgeable about many subjects.

Step Four: Reinforcing Positive Thoughts

Negative thoughts have often become so familiar that change takes persistence, consistency, and creativity. Spend some time each day working on reinforcing your positive statements (remind yourself in your daily maintenance plan). Reinforce positive responses by:

• repeating them aloud or to yourself over and over

- writing them down ten to twenty times a day

- asking someone you trust to read your positive responses to you

- making signs with the positive response, hanging them in obvious places around your home, and reading the signs every time you see them

- saying "stop" to yourself and then repeating your positive response several times every time the negative thought comes up during the day

- wearing a rubber band on your wrist, snapping it every time the negative thought comes to mind, and then repeating the positive response several times

After several weeks to months of daily reinforcement of the positive response, you will likely notice that the negative thought is no longer an issue for you. If you begin to notice the thought again, return to your daily reinforcement activities for several more days. After you feel that you have gotten one negative thought under control, go through these same exercises with other negative thoughts. There are several excellent resource books that can help you with this process. They are included in the Resources section at the end of the book.

Other Self-Esteem Exercises

Repeating Affirmations

Develop a list of positive statements about yourself or your circumstances and repeat them over and over. You can make signs or use Post-its as reminders on doors and mirrors. Following are some examples of positive affirmations:

- I am well.

- I am happy.

- My life is great.

- Lots of people like me.

- I feel great.

- I am helping my body heal itself.

- Every day, in every way, I am getting better and better and better.

- I look great.

- I have a wonderful smile.

- I do what I need to do to keep myself well.

- I eat food that nourishes me.

- I am smart.

- I can do whatever I need to do to get well and stay well.

- I can complete this task.

- I deserve all the very best that life has to offer.

- I deserve to be treated with dignity and respect at all times.

Make a list of positive affirmations that would help you feel better (including any from the list of examples that you think you'd benefit from):

_____

_____

_____

_____

Repeat these affirmations several times during the day and when you are not feeling well.

Reality Check

Checking in on what is really going on rather than responding to your initial "gut reaction" can be very helpful. For instance, if Fred comes into his house and loud music is playing, it triggers him into thinking that his son is playing the music just to annoy him. Fred's initial reaction is to get really angry with his son. Expressing this anger makes both Fred and his son feel awful. A reality check gives Fred a chance to look at what is really going on: His son thought Fred wouldn't be in until later and took advantage of the opportunity to play loud music. Instead of acting on his anger, Fred called upstairs and asked his son to turn down the music so he could rest, and his son said, "Sure!" Crisis averted.

Counting to Ten

Counting to ten is similar to a reality check. In a difficult situation, instead of responding immediately with an action that may not be in your best interest, you respond by counting to ten in your mind and then reviewing the situation. This will probably allow you to be more reasonable. For example, if Jason drops a glass of milk on the floor, his first response is usually to mutter under his breath, "I'm such a klutz!" If he counts to ten, and reviews the situation with a more positive frame of mind, he is likely to think, "I just spilled milk. That happens from time to time. No big deal."

The next chapter focuses on ways to relieve tension and stress. No matter what condition or illness you are using WRAP to work on, you can always benefit by alleviating as much stress and tension as possible.

Chapter 8

Relieving Tension
and Stress

Methods That Work to Relieve Tension

The responses in this chapter will help you relieve the tension and stress that often accompany and worsen health problems and life issues. To find those that will work best for you, try each of them several times. Note how you felt before and after you used the response to determine if it is something you want to continue using. Then practice the response daily, no matter how you feel. By doing this, you will be able to use the technique in question most effectively when you are having a difficult time. Following are a few activities that many people use to successfully relieve tension:

- Yoga: Yoga is a kind of meditative stretching and relaxing. You can learn how to do it through taking classes or reading a resource book.

- Being present in the moment: This is often referred to as mindfulness. Many of us spend so much time focusing on the future or thinking about the past that we miss out on fully experiencing what is going on in the present. Making a conscious effort to focus your attention on what you are doing right now and what is happening around you can have a very positive effect.

- Take a warm bath: This may sound simplistic, but it can help. If you are lucky enough to have access to a Jacuzzi or hot tub, it's even better. Warm water can be relaxing and healing.

- Look at something pretty or that means something special to you: Stop what you are doing and take a long close look at a flower, a leaf, a plant, the sky, a work of art, a souvenir from an adventure, a picture of a loved one, or anything else that reminds you of the beauty in your life.

- Play with children or a pet: Many people find that playing with small children and pets they enjoy can help them feel better. Romping in the grass with a dog, petting a kitten, reading a child a story, rocking a baby, and similar activities can have a calming effect, which often translates into feeling better.

Focusing

Focusing is a simple, safe, free, noninvasive yet powerful response that often helps to reduce tension. The focusing sequence uses a series of well-defined questions or steps to help focus on the "real" issue, the one of most importance at a given time. It may be different from what a person thinks is the issue or the problem. For instance, a person may be fearing that the increased intensity of their pain means a recurrence of rheumatism, when the pain is actually being intensified by tension caused by worry about a family member or a situation that is dreaded.

Once the key issue is identified, focusing can help you make the connection from the issue to the feelings generated by that issue. When the feelings are explored, the result is an understanding at a new level, which can translate into a positive change in feeling, and often, reduction of symptoms or uncomfortable feelings.

Focusing is not the same as meditation. The use of one does not preclude use of the other. In meditation, achieving stillness or an emptying of the mind is the goal. In focusing, you feel, think, respond, and gain insight.

As with any new wellness or growth-oriented technique, the more you practice it, the easier and more effective it becomes. I try to focus at least once a day to address any issues that are troubling. This helps keep them from becoming overwhelming. I do focusing exercises more often when symptoms or uncomfortable feelings worsen. Sometimes I even focus on something really good that has happened so I can linger for a time with those good feelings.

Focusing can provide:

- clarity around an issue
- increased feelings of calmness and relaxation
- feelings of overall relief
- a new level of understanding

- direction
- help in preventing distraction by less important issues
- a shift in feelings around an issue

The following is an example of focusing instructions. These instructions can be refined any way you choose to meet your individual needs. You may choose to have a person you trust, and with whom you feel safe, slowly read the instructions to you, giving you time between each step to follow the instructions in your mind and body. You do not have to say anything to the reader. Your responses are your own. If you would prefer, record the instructions, again allowing time for your thoughts, and play it to yourself when you want to do a focusing exercise. You may choose to write your responses to each step as you go along. If you continue to use focusing on a regular basis, you will eventually memorize the instructions.

1. Get ready for a focusing exercise by settling down in a comfortable space and asking yourself, "How do I feel inside my body right now?" Search around inside your body to notice any feelings of uneasiness or discomfort and focus your attention on these feelings for a few moments.

2. Ask yourself, "What's between me and feeling fine?" Try not to let your mind automatically answer; instead let the feeling that comes in your body do the answering. As each concern comes up, put it aside, making a mental list. Ask yourself, "Except for these things, am I fine?"

3. Review the list. See which problem stands out, that seems to be begging for your attention. It may be different from the one you thought was most important.

4. Ask yourself if it's okay to focus on the problem. If the answer is yes, it will feel right to you. Notice what you sense in your body when you recall the whole of that problem. (If the answer is no, it doesn't feel right to you, choose another problem that stands out and let the other alone for the time being.) Sense the whole feeling of the problem. Really feel it in your body for several minutes—focus on it.

5. Let a word, phrase, or image that matches the feeling of this problem come into your mind.

6. Go back and forth between the word, phrase, or image and the feeling in your body. Do they really match? If they don't, find another word, phrase, or image that does feel like a match. When they match, go back and forth several times between the word, phrase, or image and the feeling in your body. If the feeling in your body changes, follow it with your attention—notice it. Be with the whole of that feeling for several moments.

7. If you want, ask yourself the following questions about the problem to help facilitate a change in the way you feel:

   • How does the worst of this feel in my body?

   • What needs to happen inside me for this whole thing to change?

   • What would feel like a small step forward with all of this?

   • What would feel like a breath of fresh air in this whole thing?

   • How would it feel inside if this were all okay?

   • What needs to change inside me for this to feel better?

8. Be with the feelings that come up for a few moments. Then ask yourself, "Am I ready to stop, or should I do another round of focusing?" If you are going to stop, relax for a few minutes and notice how your feelings have changed before resuming your regular activities.

How did you feel before you did this exercise?

_____

_____

How did you feel after you did this exercise?

_____

_____

Is this an exercise you could include in your action planning? _____ y _____ n
If so, when would you include it (i.e., daily maintenance plan, early warning
signs, signs of potential crisis, or in a crisis situation)?

_____

_____

There are several resource books on focusing listed in the Resources at the
end of the book.

Relaxation and Stress Reduction Exercises

There are many relaxation and stress reduction techniques that, when used
regularly, can be excellent tools in reducing and relieving many different kinds
of symptoms and in helping increase your overall wellness. Relaxation is a skill
that is crucial to have in our fast-paced society.

Back in the early 1980s, when I first began to work intensively on addressing some problem issues in my life, I worked with a wonderful counselor who
taught me the importance of learning to relax. It was through her valuable
instruction that I became aware of the tension I had been holding in my body for
as long as I could remember. The more I practiced these techniques, the better I
felt. They put me in touch with my body in a way I had never before experienced. That class marked the beginning of a journey that is ongoing for me. I
have read countless books and attended numerous lectures and workshops, all
to enhance my wellness and reduce the feelings of tension and stress in my
body. I use these techniques regularly to enhance my overall wellness. In addition I use them as needed to put me to sleep, refresh me, help me calm down,
reduce feelings of depression, and reduce residual tension that I have from
fibromyalgia, a chronic pain disorder.

One way to learn relaxation and stress reduction techniques is to take a
course. These courses are often offered free at health care facilities. Call to
inquire about the availability of such a program in your area. Watch the local
newspaper for listings. Your counselor or "alternative" health care practitioners,
such as massage therapists, can often provide you with helpful instruction. You

can learn these skills on your own. There are excellent books and audio and video tapes available, and some of these may be available at your local library or bookstore (see Resources).

You may find that a relaxation tape helps you to achieve a deeper state of relaxation. These tapes are available for sale. They often feature relaxing music or nature sounds in the background. An inexpensive option is to record your own tape with your favorite relaxing music in the background. Use one of the many exercises in resource books or develop an exercise that feels good to you.

It's hard to learn to relax when you are in the midst of a crisis or when you are experiencing more severe symptoms. It is best to learn how to relax when you are feeling well. Then it will be there as a resource to help you feel better when times are more difficult.

Practice relaxation daily at a regular time. You will figure out for yourself the times when your house is most quiet and you would be able to take a fifteen minute (or longer) break without interruption. Ask others in your household to respect this time by being quiet and not disturbing you. If you miss a time now and again, don't fret. Just do the best you can. Practice relaxing until it becomes second nature and you can use it anytime you begin to feel nervous, tense, or irritable.

Often people fall asleep when they are doing relaxation exercises. That's fine. You may even decide to use these exercises to help you fall asleep at night or get back to sleep if you are awakened. If you fall asleep when you are doing your relaxation exercises, it just means you were probably really tired. However, one of the goals of these exercises is to teach your body to hold less tension throughout the day as you are involved in your activities, so try to do at least one relaxation exercise each day where you don't fall asleep.

Locate a space or several spaces in your home that are cozy, comfortable, and quiet, where you can be away from the concerns of your life and you can do your relaxation and stress reduction exercises. It may be in your bedroom or living room. Relaxing outdoors in a secluded place in the woods, in a meadow, by the ocean, or on a mountain top (or even in your backyard, if it is peaceful and private) is also a good idea.

When you notice uncomfortable feelings or symptoms, spend more time using your relaxation techniques and do them more often during the day. At these times, it is helpful to use an audio or video tape with a guided relaxation exercise.

Try some of the following relaxation exercises. See which ones help you feel better. (If any of these exercises make you feel worse, stop doing the exercise and try a different one).

Breathing Awareness

Lie down on the floor with your legs flat or bent at the knees, your arms at your sides palms up, and your eyes closed. Breathe through your nose if you can. Focus on your breathing. Place your hand on the place that seems to rise and fall the most as you breathe. If this place is on your chest, you need to practice breathing more deeply so that your abdomen rises and falls most noticeably. When nervous or anxious, people tend to breathe short, shallow breaths in the upper chest. Now place both hands on your abdomen and notice how your abdomen rises and falls with each breath. Notice if your chest is moving in harmony with your abdomen. Continue to do this for several minutes. Get up slowly. This is something you can do during a break at work. If you can't lie down, you can do it sitting in a chair.

How did you feel before you did this exercise?

_____

_____

How did you feel after you did this exercise?

_____

_____

Is this an exercise you could include in your action planning? _____ y _____ n
If so, when would you include it (i.e., daily maintenance plan, early warning signs, signs of potential crisis, or in a crisis situation)?

_____

_____

_____

Deep Breathing

This exercise can be practiced in a variety of positions. However, it is most effective if you can do it lying down with your knees bent and your spine straight. After lying down, scan your body for tension. Place one hand on your abdomen and one hand on your chest. Inhale slowly and deeply through your nose into your abdomen to push up your hand as much as feels comfortable. Your chest should only move a little in response to the movement in your abdomen.

When you feel at ease with your breathing, inhale through your nose and exhale through your mouth, making a relaxing whooshing sound as you gently blow out. This will relax your mouth, tongue, and jaw. Continue taking long, slow, deep breaths that raise and lower your abdomen. As you become more and more relaxed, focus on the sound and feeling of your breathing. Continue this deep breathing for five or ten minutes at a time, once or twice a day. At the end of each session, scan your body for tension. As you become used to this exercise, you can practice it wherever you happen to be in a standing, sitting, or lying position. Use it whenever you feel tense.

How did you feel before you did this exercise?

_____

_____

How did you feel after you did this exercise?

_____

_____

Is this an exercise you could include in your action planning? _____ y _____ n
If so, when would you include it (i.e., daily maintenance plan, early warning
signs, signs of potential crisis, or in a crisis situation)?

_____

_____

The Inner Exploration

Pick a part of your body on which to focus all your attention. Explore that
part of your body in detail with your mind. What are the sensations in this
part of your body? How does it move? What does it do? Is it tense? If it is
tense, practice relaxing this part of the body by imagining that it is feeling very
warm, soft, and light. It also helps to repeat over and over in your mind: "My
_____ (name the body part or parts) is/are very comfort-
able and relaxed." You may want to choose parts of your body that tend to be
tense such as the neck, shoulders, jaw, forehead, or lower back. Or you may
choose internal areas that tend to be tense such as the stomach or chest. Another
idea is to focus on body parts that you rarely think about, such as your toes,
your elbows, or behind your knees.

How did you feel before you did this exercise?

_____

_____

How did you feel after you did this exercise?

_____

_____

Is this an exercise you could include in your action planning? _____ y _____ n
If so, when would you include it (i.e., daily maintenance plan, early warning
signs, signs of potential crisis, or in a crisis situation)?

_____

_____

Being Present in the Moment

Most of the stress in our lives comes from thinking about the past or worrying about the future. When all of your attention is focused in the present moment or on what you are doing right now, there is no room to feel anything else. When meditating, all of your attention is focused on the present moment. When other thoughts intrude, just turn your awareness back to the present. It is not necessary to be alone in a special place to focus all your attention on the moment. Try doing it when you are feeling irritated, waiting in a line, stopped at a street light, stuck in traffic, or feeling overwhelmed or worried. Try to fully experience things just as they are, without expectations. Notice how this makes you feel.

How did you feel before you did this exercise?

_____

_____

How did you feel after you did this exercise?

_____

_____

Is this an exercise you could include in your action planning? _____ y _____ n
If so, when would you include it (i.e., daily maintenance plan, early warning signs, signs of potential crisis, or in a crisis situation)?

_____

_____

Progressive Relaxation

The purpose of this technique is to get you to focus on body sensations and how relaxation feels by systematically tensing and then relaxing the muscle groups of your body. You may want to make a tape recording of this exercise so you can use it when you need to. Be sure you leave yourself time on the tape to tense and relax your muscles. You can also purchase an already made tape (see Resources).

Find a quiet space where you will not be disturbed. You can do it either lying on your back or sitting in a chair, as long as you are comfortable. Close your eyes. Now clench your right fist as tightly as you can. Be aware of the tension as you do so. Keep it clenched for a moment. Now relax. Feel the looseness in your right hand and compare it to the tension you felt previously. Tense your right fist again, then relax it, and again, notice the difference.

Now clench your left fist as tightly as you can. Be aware of the tension as you do so. Keep it clenched for a moment. Now relax. Feel the looseness in your left hand and compare it to the tension you felt previously. Tense your left fist again, relax it, and notice the difference.

Bend your elbows and tense your biceps as hard as you can. Notice the feeling of tightness. Relax and straighten out your arms. Let the relaxation flow through your arms and compare it to the tightness you felt previously. Tense and relax your biceps again.

Wrinkle your forehead as tightly as you can. Now relax it and let it smooth out. Feel your forehead and scalp becoming relaxed. Now frown and notice the tension spreading through your forehead again. Relax and allow your forehead to become smooth.

Close your eyes now and squint them very tightly. Feel the tension. Now relax your eyes. Tense and relax your eyes again. Now let them remain gently closed.

Now clench your jaw, bite hard, and feel the tension through your jaw. Now relax your jaw. Your lips should be slightly parted. Notice the difference. Clench and relax again. Press your tongue against the roof of your mouth. Now relax. Do this again. Press and purse your lips together. Now relax them. Repeat this. Feel the relaxation throughout your forehead, scalp, eyes, jaw, tongue, and lips.

Hold your head back as far as it can comfortably go and observe the tightness in the neck. Roll it to the right and notice how the tension moves and changes. Roll your head to the left and notice how the tension moves and changes. Now straighten your head and bring it forward, pressing your chin against your chest. Notice the tension in your throat and the back of your neck. Now relax and allow your shoulders to return to a comfortable position. Allow yourself to feel more and more relaxed. Now shrug your shoulders and hunch your head down between them. Relax your shoulders. Allow them to drop back and feel the relaxation moving through your neck, throat, and shoulders. Feel the deep relaxation. Give your whole body a chance to relax. Feel how comfortable and heavy it is.

Now breathe in and fill your lungs completely. Hold your breath and notice the tension. Now let your breath out and let your chest become loose. Continue relaxing, breathing gently in and out. Repeat this breathing several times and notice the tension draining out of your body.

Tighten your stomach and hold the tightness. Feel the tension. Now relax your stomach. Now place your hand on your stomach. Breathe deeply into your stomach, pushing your hand up. Hold for a moment and then relax. Now arch your back without straining, keeping the rest of your body as relaxed as possible. Notice the tension in your lower back. Now relax deeper and deeper.

Tighten your buttocks and then relax them. Flex your thighs by pressing your heels down as hard as you can. Now relax and notice the difference. Do this again. Now curl your toes down, making your calves tense. Notice the tension. Now relax. Bend your toes toward your face, creating tension in your shins. Relax and notice the difference.

Feel the heaviness throughout your lower body as the relaxation gets deeper and deeper. Relax your feet, ankles, calves, shins, knees, thighs, and buttocks. Now let the relaxation spread to your stomach, lower back, and chest. Let go more and more. Experience deeper and deeper relaxation in your shoulders, arms, and hands, deeper and deeper. Notice the feeling of looseness and relaxation in your neck, jaws, and all your facial muscles. Now just relax and be aware of how your whole body feels before you return to your other activities.

How did you feel before you did this exercise?

_____

_____

How did you feel after you did this exercise?

_____

_____

Is this an exercise you could include in your action planning? _____ y _____ n If so, when would you include it (i.e., daily maintenance plan, early warning signs, signs of potential crisis, or in a crisis situation)?

_____

_____

Guided Imagery

Guided imagery uses your imagination to direct your focus in a way that is relaxing and healing. Try the following guided imagery meditation. Get in a comfortable sitting or lying position. Make sure you are warm enough but not too warm and that you will not be interrupted by the phone or the needs of others.

Stare at a spot above your head on the ceiling. Take a deep breath in to a count of eight, hold it for a count of four, let it out for a count of eight. Do that two more times. Now close your eyes, but keep them in the same position they were in when you were staring at the spot on the ceiling. Breathe in to a count of eight, hold for a count of four, breathe out for a count of eight.

Now focus on your toes. Let them completely relax. Now move the relaxation slowly up your legs, through your heels and calves to your knees. Now let the warm feeling of relaxation move up your thighs. Feel your whole lower body relaxing. Let the relaxation move very slowly through your buttocks, lower abdomen, and lower back. Now feel it moving very slowly up your spine and through your abdomen. Now feel the warm relaxation flowing into your chest and upper back.

Let this relaxation flow from your shoulders, down your arms, through your elbows and wrists, out through your hands and fingers. Now let the relaxation go slowly through your throat and up your neck, letting it all soften and relax. Let it move up into your face. Feel the relaxation fill your jaw and cheek muscles, and then the area around your eyes. Let it move up into your forehead. Now let your whole scalp relax and feel warm and comfortable. Your body should now be completely relaxed with the warm feeling of relaxation filling every muscle and cell of your body.

Now picture yourself walking on a sandy beach during a sunny day. As you stroll along, you feel the warmth of the sun on your back. You lay down on the sand. The sand cradles you and feels warm and comfortable on your back. The sun warms your body. You hear the waves crashing against the shore in a steady rhythm. The sound of sea gulls calling overhead adds to your feeling of blissful contentment.

As you lay here, you realize that you are perfectly and completely relaxed. You feel safe and at peace with the world. You know you have the power to relax yourself completely at any time. You know that by completely relaxing, you are giving your body the opportunity to stabilize itself, and that when you wake up you will feel calm and relaxed, and that you will be able to get on with your tasks for the day. Then, slowly wiggle your fingers and toes. Gradually open your eyes and resume your activities.

How did you feel before you did this exercise?

_____

_____

How did you feel after you did this exercise?

_____

_____

Is this an exercise you could include in your action planning? _____ y _____ n
If so, when would you include it (i.e., daily maintenance plan, early warning signs, signs of potential crisis, or in a crisis situation)?

_____

_____

Auralizing

Roby Adkisson, a woman I met at a workshop in Iowa who has been searching for relaxation techniques, shared with me the technique of auralizing. It works well for people who have a hard time doing visualization exercises. It also works well for people who find music to be very relaxing but can't use it in some places—like in airports, in waiting rooms, or when having certain medical procedures. Adkisson explains:

> I'm not good at visualizing at all. My strongest sense is my sense of hearing. So when I do relaxation exercises, I do something which I call "auralizing." This is hearing in one's mind, analogous to visualizing, which involves seeing in one's mind. I've had the ability to auralize for years, without ever having a name for it. I auralize music, which I dearly love. I can auralize my favorite pieces of music in my head, and this relaxes me, just as much as actually listening to music does.

To try auralizing, first identify several pieces of music you really enjoy. It will help if this music is already on a tape or compact disc that you own or plan to purchase. Listen to your selected pieces several times. Then sit down in a comfortable place where you will not be distracted. Without the music playing, practice hearing the pieces over and over in your head. Do this several times daily until you are comfortable with the technique. This technique is a particularly good one to use when you awaken in the night and have difficulty getting back to sleep.

How did you feel before you did this exercise?

_____

_____

How did you feel after you did this exercise?

_____

_____

Is this an exercise you could include in your action planning? _____ y _____ n
If so, when would you include it (i.e., daily maintenance plan, early warning signs, signs of potential crisis, or in a crisis situation)?

_____

_____

Affecting the Senses

Things that affect your senses—of smell, sight, hearing, taste, and touch—can have a strong impact on how you feel. Consider the following actions that you can take to affect your senses in a positive way. Then use the ones that you think would be helpful as part of your WRAP.

Using Aromatherapy

Exposing yourself to something that smells good to you can make you feel better, and the effects of particular smells on how you feel shouldn't be discounted. Sometimes a bouquet of fragrant flowers, like lilacs, in the house or the smell of a fresh baked loaf of bread will help you feel better.

Many people have discovered fragrances that help them feel good. Usually places that sell natural fragrances, like health food stores, health spas, and natural pharmacies, have testers so you can smell the one that is right for you. They come in a variety of forms including room scents, perfume oils, lotions, body oil blends, bath products, and hair products. Most people find the natural fragrances preferable to synthetic—try and look for essential oils as opposed to fragrances for the optimum effect.

The best way to learn about using these fragrances is to check them out in a good resource book or consult with an aromatherapy specialist. Don't necessarily take the word of a shop owner who is anxious to sell a product. It's very individual. You have to choose a scent that fits you. You also change scents by season or by your mood.

Responding Visually

Certain colors and the appearance of your surrounding environment can help you feel better. Surround yourself with colors and things that you enjoy looking at. The following suggestions may give you some ideas:

- Wear your favorite colors.

- Do some redecorating with colors you enjoy (if cost is an issue, check out your local thrift store for colorful curtains and spreads, or try dyeing something).

- Adorn your walls with pictures you enjoy.

- Have beautiful fresh flowers in your living space as often as possible.

- Visit scenic places.

Getting a Massage

Help yourself feel even more cool, calm, and collected by giving your skin a treat. Have a massage by a skilled professional, give yourself a massage, or ask your partner or a good friend to give you a massage. It can also be relaxing to rub your skin with a rich oil or lotion.

Listening to Music

Pay attention to your sense of hearing by pampering yourself with delightful music you really enjoy. Find a good music store where you can listen to music before you purchase it. Libraries often have records and tapes available for loan. If you enjoy music, make it an essential part of every day.

I often conduct workshops on developing WRAPs. As part of the workshop, participants share the symptom responses that work for them. Music is the one mentioned most often. People of all ages seem to appreciate the recuperative value of music. Listening to music and making music help people feel better.

Cheryl Coplan, a college professor who teaches people how to use music as a wellness tool, has used music in her own life and in working with others to address a variety of emotional symptoms. She says:

> Listening to music may enhance your sense of well-being. The key point to think about is how does the music you listen to help you. Are you listening to music for a specific purpose? Maybe you find that soft instrumental and flute music can be very relaxing and a way of managing stress. Some people find classical music effective for calming their anxiety. But for others, classical music can be as energizing as

bouncy drum music. So, before you turn on the music, ask yourself what type of music you like, how it affects your mood, and what kind of mood you are currently wanting to facilitate.

In addition, don't overlook the benefits of making your own music. Plastic or wooden recorders are relatively inexpensive, and if you learn just the pentatonic scale (tones *do, re, me, sol,* and *la*) any arrangement of the tones will sound pleasing to your ear.

Think about the kinds of music that make you feel better. I enjoy upbeat folk music, certain classical pieces and piano music. Others like jazz, big band, classical, opera, rock, easy listening, gospel, or new age selections. You may prefer listening to musical instruments or vocals. The kind of instrument that predominates may affect the way you feel. List the kinds of music you enjoy, how they make you feel, and the names of your favorite selections.

Make sure you keep these selections readily accessible. Have available tapes or compact discs or know the local stations that feature music you enjoy. I keep my favorite compact discs along with my personal disc player in a basket next to my easy chair. If your music disturbs other people in your living space, consider getting ear phones and a personal tape player or disc player so that your music is available to you when you need it. When you are noticing uncomfortable feelings or symptoms, spend some time during the day listening to these kinds of music.

Making Music

Making music is also a good way to release feelings and pent-up emotions. Drumming and other kinds of rhythm instruments are becoming more and more popular as a way to relieve tension and increase well-being. Or perhaps you have an instrument that you enjoy playing like the piano, a guitar, or the saxophone. If making music appeals to you and increases your sense of well-being, take time to do it. Use it in developing your action plans. Remember you don't have to play perfectly or even well to enjoy playing. You don't need anyone else to critique for you. Just play for the sake of playing, for the fun of it.

I enjoy beating out the rhythm of a favorite song on a drum. Drums are great for this purpose. Put on some of your favorite music and then just beat to the rhythm. Enjoy yourself. If you don't have a drum, find something that it is okay to beat a rhythm on and use that.

Sing

Singing increases well-being. It fills your lungs with fresh air and makes you feel better. Sing to yourself. Sing at the top of your lungs. Sing when you are driving your car. Sing when you are in the shower. Sing when you are having a difficult treatment. Sing for the fun of it. Sing along with favorite records, tapes, compact discs, or the radio. Sing the favorite songs you remember from your childhood.

Cheryl Coplan says:

Remember that you can use your voice to make music. It doesn't matter how well you can carry a tune or what quality of voice you have, singing expands your body and contributes to your recovery and wellness.

In the next chapter, you will be given ideas on how to customize your WRAP to address any special needs or circumstances you have.

Chapter 9

Adapting WRAP for Special Needs and Circumstances

By using your creative skills and those of the people in your support network, your WRAP can easily be adapted for use by people who have special needs or who are dealing with difficult situations. Because each person's circumstances and experience are so unique, it is impossible to accurately describe how your WRAP can be tailored to meet your individual needs. However, in this chapter you will get some ideas for addressing special needs, difficult circumstances for which you have some advanced warning, and serious events for which you have no warning.

Addressing Special Needs

Jane Winterling has worked with people in developing plans for people with special needs. She says:

> These plans can look very different for people with special needs. For example, people who have the cluster of symptoms commonly referred to as schizophrenia often have very few or no triggering events. Other people, who have experienced trauma or who have an illness like arthritis, may have very long lists of triggers. Their crisis comes from

not recognizing triggers and not having good response plans to address them.

Your WRAP can be as long or as short as is practical. It may contain only one item and a single response in each section. It can be tape recorded, written in Braille, or be a series of illustrative pictures instead of words—let your imagination and your needs be your guide. The following list includes some examples of the kinds of special needs and circumstances that some people need to consider when developing a WRAP:

- blindness
- being nonverbal
- having severe pain
- illiteracy
- homelessness
- feeling you have to be told what to do
- being an adolescent
- poverty
- institutionalization

- deafness
- being physically disabled
- developmental disabilities
- inability to write
- low self-esteem
- debilitation from severe illness or injuries
- being of an advanced age
- limited access to health care
- court-ordered care

The following examples may give you some ideas for dealing with special needs when you are working on your own plan.

Cassie

Cassie is twenty. She has been blind since birth. She wanted to set up a WRAP to help build her self-esteem. She felt that her low self-esteem was keeping her from making friends and working toward her goal of being a social worker. Written materials are not an option for Cassie. While she has a reader several hours a week, she felt that restricting her access to her WRAP to those times when her reader was available would limit its usefulness. She decided there were two ways she could develop her plan. One would be to develop the plan in Braille, a skill she learned as a child. The other would be to record it. She decided to try recording it, remembering that if that didn't feel comfortable, she could try it in braille.

She found it quite easy to record the plan. As tapes are quite inexpensive, she decided it would be best to have each section on a separate tape so she wouldn't have to search for the section she needed. She labeled the tapes with Braille labels and kept them together in a box, keeping it on an accessible shelf so it was always available for easy review.

Now, each morning as she eats her breakfast, she listens to her recording of her daily maintenance plan to remind her of the things she needs to do that day. She also reviews the tapes about her triggers and early warning signs, so that she will be aware of them if they come up during the day. If they do, she listens to the tapes again to remind herself of the actions she needs to take to keep her feelings about herself from becoming more negative. Cassie is finding that she is quickly memorizing her daily maintenance list, triggers, early warning signs, and response plans, making it easy to take quick action (described in her tape about potential crisis) to keep herself from feeling really badly about herself. Cassie did not develop a crisis plan because she did not feel it was necessary in dealing with her current issue.

Janet

Janet had a debilitating stroke when she was thirty-four. It took away her ability to speak or write and left her with multiple physical handicaps. In working with Janet, her therapists became aware that she was highly motivated to reduce her disabilities. They described the WRAP process to her, and she indicated she was very interested in developing such a plan for herself. In this case, the therapists made suggestions to her about her symptoms and responses. She nodded if she wanted to use them and shook her head to indicate a negative response. The therapists wrote the plan for her and reviewed it with her daily and as needed throughout the day.

Brian

Because of a birth injury that limited his ability to learn, Brian, age twenty-five, is unable to read. He has trouble doing things to keep himself healthy. He also finds some circumstances frightening and the accompanying agitation makes it hard for him to do things for himself. Working with his case manager, he developed a WRAP using pictures cut from magazines and simple drawings as reminders.

His daily maintenance list contains a picture of someone taking a shower (reminder of personal hygiene tasks), a healthy breakfast (reminding him to eat his breakfast), a boy riding a bicycle (reminding him to exercise), and a picture of a busy street with a black *X* across it (a reminder to avoid going into the busy section of town where he gets disoriented and frightened).

His list of triggers includes a picture with lots of traffic and a picture of a crowd of people. If he inadvertently finds himself in either of these situations, he finds he can reduce his anxiety by taking some deep breaths and leaving the area, illustrated with pictures of a woman in a resting yoga pose and a picture of a shady, private place. An early warning sign for Brian is if he is feeling angry and irritable, illustrated with a picture of a man who is clearly in a foul mood. Brian is reminded by the picture of a phone and a picture of a walking path that this is a good time to call one of his friends and take a long walk.

If Brian finds that he is feeling hostile and his grooming is poor—these problems are illustrated with pictures in his early warning signs section—Brian calls his case manager to ask for advice, calls a friend, and chooses a favorite video game to play for the evening.

Brian's case manager worked with him on his crisis plan, writing it out and giving him copies to give to his supporters. Brian feels he is in a crisis when he is shouting at people and trying to destroy property. In this circumstance, he wants his supporters to restrain him as gently as possible and talk to him in a reassuring manner until he calms down. Then he wants them to play ball or watch a TV show with him.

Mark

Mark has been living on the streets for three months, spending the nights at a neighborhood shelter for the homeless. He was evicted from his apartment after he lost his job as a night watchman in a small industrial plant that shut down. He is feeling very discouraged and is finding that he lacks the motivation to take action that would help him to get a job and improve his circumstances. Cold weather is coming and he knows he will have to move to a warmer climate—leaving behind a few close friends whom he treasures—if he doesn't find work soon.

He talked to a worker at the shelter about his concerns. The worker suggested he develop a WRAP and volunteered to work with him on it. The worker agreed to supply an inexpensive spiral notebook, to store it safely at the shelter during the day, and to review it with Mark each day before Mark begins his day. He also helped Mark get some clothes from a thrift store that would be suitable for interviews.

Mark's daily maintenance plan included tasks like taking a shower, shampooing, getting a healthy meal at the soup kitchen, and making at least one job contact. A trigger he has identified is being turned down for a job. Instead of going off alone and sulking, he found that if he talked to one of several friends about the experience, it didn't leave him feeling so unmotivated. His early warning signs included feeling unmotivated and isolated and craving alcohol. When he notices these symptoms, he goes to Alcoholics Anonymous at least twice during the day and takes a long run along the river. Mark knows things are breaking down (potential crisis) when he avoids making his daily job contact, avoids his friends, and stops eating. When this happens, he goes to Alcoholics Anonymous three times during the day, stays with his friends, and contacts his counselor at the local mental health center.

Symptoms of a crisis were that he was not taking any action—just sitting and staring for more than six hours. In this circumstance, he asked his friends to stay with him, keep him from drinking, and listen if he felt like talking.

Addressing Difficult Changes in Life Circumstances

There are times in life when you will have special needs due to a sudden change in your circumstances. You may be doing very well and suddenly you get "thrown a curve ball." Sometimes you have advance warning and sometimes you don't. These times are very hard. To keep things from getting out of control during these times—which causes you and others even more difficulty and pain—you need information, help, and support from others.

Advance Warning of Hard Times to Come

There are some very difficult times for which you have advance warning that, while never easy, can be ameliorated from planning and preparation. These include:

- learning that you are going to become severely disabled—blind, deaf, physically debilitated, etc.

- learning that you have a very serious life-threatening or terminal illness—AIDS, cancer, multiple sclerosis, Alzheimer's, Parkinson's disease, etc.

- finding out that a close family member is going to become severely disabled or has a serious, life-threatening, or terminal illness

Use the advance planning worksheet (there is a copy of this form at the end of this section and in the appendix) to help you think about and organize your efforts to keep yourself as well as possible and reduce the stress in your life during this hard time. If the difficult time is limited, the advance planning worksheet may be enough to guide you through it. If you are going to be dealing with this situation for a long time, you may want to make some changes in and additions to your entire WRAP. In this way, you can minimize the effects of this situation on your life as much as possible and decrease the likelihood that this situation will worsen other health and/or emotional problems.

Following are some examples of how people adapted their WRAP to assist them through a time of difficulty that came with advanced warning.

Marty

When Marty found out three close family members were dying of cancer, he thought "this is going to be the end of me." All the time he had put into working on his depression and arthritis—all the improvements to his wellness that he had made—felt like they were going to disappear. Through acknowledging that this was going to be a very difficult time in his life and making and following his WRAP, he has been able to minimize the impact of this situation on every aspect of his life. It has enabled him to cope more effectively so he can be available, supportive, and helpful to those he loves.

Justin

Justin was told that he had a malignant tumor that needed to be removed. He would need chemotherapy following the surgery, and the eventual outcome was unclear and would not be known for some time. This kind of a serious event would cause anyone to panic initially. The worry and dread caused by such a diagnosis and prognosis might cause long-term anxiety or depression, and could even reduce his chances at recovery. Once he got over the initial shock, he determined that he would take some assertive action in his own behalf to achieve the highest levels of wellness possible at all times. His first task was to educate himself. He searched the internet and the local library for information, and then he followed up on leads with letters, phone calls, and e-mail. Through that search he developed a daily maintenance plan that he felt would work for him. It included:

- following a special diet developed by a nutritionist/physician specializing in the treatment of the kind of cancer he had

- an intensive stress reduction and relaxation regime that he learned by taking a course at the local hospital

- spending at least one hour every day with close family members and friends who are supportive and fun to be with
- taking a daily walk for at least half an hour whenever his condition allowed
- spending a minimum of one hour each day involved in one of several creative activities that he enjoys
- spending at least fifteen minutes each day writing in his journal

Following is Justin's list for signs of potential crisis (when things are breaking down).

Things I must do:

- call my doctor or other health care professional; ask for and follow their instructions
- call and talk to one of my supporters for as long as needed
- arrange for someone to stay with me around the clock until my symptoms subside
- take action so I cannot hurt myself if my symptoms get worse (e.g., give my medications, check book, credit cards, and car keys to a previously designated friend for safe keeping)
- make sure I am doing everything on my daily maintenance plan
- arrange and take at least three days off from any responsibilities
- have at least two peer counseling sessions daily
- do three deep breathing relaxation exercises
- do two focusing exercises
- write in my journal for at least one half hour

Choices of things he could do if it felt right to him:

- creative activities
- exercise
- play with the dog or cat

Following are questions he could ask himself.

Do I need:

- a physical examination
- a medication check
- a medication change
- extra protection for myself
- to stop driving

- to reassess my situation and make some changes

- to get away for a few days

- to call or see my doctor

- to see a health care specialist

- to ask for extra time with my counselor

- a massage

- a sauna or whirlpool

He also had a reminder to ask others to do tasks that are particularly hard. The tasks he needed help with included:

- getting the car repaired

- cleaning the house

- mowing the lawn

- raking up all the leaves

- shoveling the snow off the driveway

He made a list of things he could do to prepare himself for the time when he would have less energy. Because of his circumstances, Justin added a special list of things he needed to do right away to the beginning of his daily maintenance plan. These were tasks that he felt would simplify his upcoming treatment and recovery and things that he would only need to do once or several times. These things included:

- purchase two comfortable, easy-care outfits and extra underwear and socks

- have car and home maintenance tasks taken care of

- have plenty of easy-to-prepare meals on hand

- make a list of all those responsibilities I don't want to neglect (e.g., caring for children or pets, paying bills, and weekly calls to my aged parents)

As he completed each task, he crossed it off the list. Although times like this are always very difficult, Justin knew that making some advanced preparations could reduce stress for him and his family during this difficult time.

Nancy

Nancy, who had been using her WRAP in dealing with her arthritis, learned that her husband had two concurrent terminal illnesses: lupus and cancer. It was expected that he would live several more years, but that during that time his health would gradually decline. After she got over the shock of this dire prognosis, she decided that it was important to take some action while her husband was still doing fairly well. This included things that might become necessary but be more difficult to address after the illness had progressed, things that would help her stay well through this difficult time, and things that would enhance both of their lives in the remaining time they had to spend together.

She conferred with family members and friends and revised her plan. Some of the changes would necessitate using money that had been saved for other purposes, but she decided the actions were so important that her priorities needed to change and the money needed to be spent. By the time the situation had become very serious, she was ready. It wasn't easy, but it was much easier than it might have been. The actions she took included:

- educating herself and family members through research and attendance at support groups so they knew what to expect

- making sure she had plenty of good support to be with her through this difficult time (she invited friends to a luncheon, described the situation, and explained to them what they could do to be supportive of her)

- arranging for family members and friends to provide her husband with some care so she could take time to do things she enjoys and to do the things on her daily maintenance plan

- taking a meditation course and scheduling daily time for meditation

- stocking up on canned and frozen foods, cleaning supplies, and paper products, to avoid emergency shopping trips

- purchasing ample supplies of night wear, undergarments, shoes, and easy-care outfits for herself and her husband so choosing and caring for clothing would not become stressful

- making sure the family vehicles were in good working order and at least half full of gas at all times so she wouldn't have to worry about it in a crisis situation

- taking care of personal health maintenance chores—annual physical, dental work, eye examination, etc.

- contracting renovations to their home that would make things easy, convenient, and accessible for her husband (i.e., wide doorways, ramps, levers on doors to make them easy to open, and grab bars in the bathroom)

- making major purchases that would increase levels of ease and comfort for both of them, like a television with a remote control, lounge chairs, and comfortable outdoor furniture

- listing easy, enjoyable day trips and other activities that could be used on good days to increase the quality of the time they had left to spend together

- making arrangements with family members to insure that someone was always with her husband during important medical consultations so instructions and recommendations were clear

When things got really tough, Nancy found it helpful to repeat over and over the serenity prayer: "God grant me the ability to change the things I can change, to accept the things I cannot change, and the wisdom to know the difference." Now, several years after her husband's death, she says that the advance planning was a lifesaver for her throughout his illness.

Adapting Your WRAP

Is there a circumstance in your life that could benefit from advance planning?
y _____ n _____ If so, describe:

_____

_____

The following advance planning worksheet can help you get through this difficult time. There is a copy of this in the appendix that you can reproduce. Making this plan is not easy to do, especially when you are already under a lot of
stress. Ask family members and friends for help.

Advance Planning Worksheet

Describe anticipated event or circumstance

_____

_____

When will it occur, or when is it likely to occur?

_____

What actions could you take in advance to ease the situation and when could
you take them?

_____

_____

_____

_____

(Focus on one action at a time for the following questions. Use photocopies of
this form to address each action possible.) Who will you need to ask for help to
get this done?

_____

_____

_____

How will you implement this action?

_____

_____

How will taking this action help?

What purchases need to be made?

If you don't have the money readily available to make these purchases, how could you make this happen (credit cards, loan from a bank or family member, savings, grants from local or government organizations, etc.)?

Put the copies in your WRAP binder.

Sudden Loss or Disaster

There are many extremely difficult situations that can occur in your life for which you get no warning, such as the loss of a loved one, the loss of your home and all your personal possessions to a fire, or having your whole town wiped out by a natural disaster. These might be referred to as "what ifs." Many people are quite adept at developing an extensive list of "what ifs." These are the kind of things that keep some people awake at night, doing what is known as "catastrophizing." Because many people obsess about these kinds of things too much already, most of which will never happen, it is not useful to list them.

While it is not useful to focus too much about things you cannot control or predict, it can be useful to people who worry to know, in the back of their minds, that if one of these difficult situations occurred, their WRAP could help them prevent a personal crisis or a worsening of their other symptoms (the ones for which they are using their WRAP in the first place).

Read the following suggested guidelines for dealing with a difficult situation for which you have no warning. Mark those that you think would be helpful for you, adding any others you can think of that you may find helpful in an unexpected crisis. Insert it in your WRAP binder.

❏   Do everything on your daily maintenance plan every day. You may want to increase or change the use of some things on your daily maintenance plan. For instance, you may want to increase the amount of time you meditate, exercise, or talk with a supporter.

❏ Refer to the plan you developed for responding to triggers and increase the number or duration of some activities in the plan. You could even add any new activities you have read about in this book but haven't yet tried. You may want to spend extra time each day talking to supportive friends and peer counseling. Depending on the situation, you might benefit from extra time with a member of the clergy or a counselor. Meditation time could be increased. Additional focusing exercises might help. You may need to remind yourself to keep the house organized if your life has become very chaotic.

❏ If you are experiencing early warning signs, check over that list and see which of those activities might be used or increased to help you feel better.

❏ If you feel that things are breaking down and that your wellness is being compromised, refer to you WRAP response plan, increasing activities as necessary. If the following are not part of your WRAP, consider using them:

- Take very good care of yourself and treat yourself as if you were your own best friend.

- Reach out for whatever support you find most comforting (spiritual support, therapy, time with family and/or friends).

- See your doctor and/or counselor. Ask for a medication change or supplementation if warranted.

- Ask for additional support from family members and friends.

- Ask for help with daily tasks.

- Take time off from work.

- Do problem solving exercises or brainstorming to help you in decision making at this hard time.

- Keep your crisis plan updated to keep you in control even when it seems as if things are out of control.

Using these guidelines and others you have thought of, develop a list of things that you feel would help you if you found yourself in an extremely difficult situation with no advance warning. Insert at the end of the crisis section of your binder.

In case of a sudden loss or disaster with no warning, I think the following would be helpful to me:

_____

_____

_____

_____

_____

Chapter 10

Using WRAP in Working with Individuals and Groups: A Chapter for Health Care Providers

Helping Others Develop a WRAP

If you are in a helping profession—a case manager, counselor, therapist, social worker, doctor—you can help and support another person in developing their WRAP. You may do this with a group of people or with individuals. Whether you are working with individuals or groups, there are some general guidelines you need to follow. In addition, there are some specific strategies that will assist you in this work.

General Guidelines

- As a helper, you can make suggestions and share observations and ideas. Do not *require* anyone to do anything. Do not tell them what to do or what to write. This would violate the basic premise that this action plan is developed by the person who will be using it. If you can't think of anything to say, just listen. Let the person or people know that this is what you are doing.

- Avoid correcting spelling and grammar. They are not important in this planning process and might inhibit the person who is developing the plan.

- Treat the person who is developing the WRAP with dignity, compassion, and respect at all times.

- Help to develop the WRAP at a pace that is comfortable for the individual who is developing the plan. Avoid setting rigid time schedules around development or completion of the plan. Some parts of the plan are difficult for people because they remind them of hard times in the past or because they have not been aware of the cause-and-effect relationships between life circumstances and symptoms or hard times. They should work on their WRAP only as long as they feel comfortable. Then put it away for another time. For many people, developing a WRAP is like discovering that the world is round when you thought it was flat, and it takes some time to get used to the idea.

- There is no right or wrong way to develop a plan—unless it is injurious to the person. People should feel free to customize the plan in any way that most effectively meets their needs. At the same time, it is important to be realistic. People may have a hard time recognizing symptoms until they become very severe. If someone tries to tell you that having pain so severe that they can't walk or being semiconscious is an early warning sign, you can gently but firmly disagree and suggest that these may be more appropriately labeled as crisis situations.

- Always give the person or people you are working with a message of hope. No one can predict the course of anyone else's illness or situation. Sometimes the most difficult cases turn out very well.

- Encourage personal responsibility and self-advocacy.

- Do not judge, criticize, blame, or shame the person you are working with. This never helps and always makes it difficult for the person to have high self-esteem, self-advocate, or take personal responsibility.

- Use a tone of voice and body language that is encouraging and supportive. If your frustration and feelings of helplessness overwhelm you, shorten the session and set up another time to continue this work. Get some support for yourself. If working with this person or group of people is too hard for you, find someone else to take over.

- Set up a relationship with the person you are working with that focuses on equality and mutuality, rather than on a hierarchical system where the health care provider is assumed to be the expert. Keep in mind that no one knows more about this situation, whatever it may be, than the person who is experiencing it.

Keep in mind that for many years, and particularly with certain types of illness or circumstances, there has been an implication that the individual has done something wrong or bad and is to blame for the illness or circumstance. Also, many treatments can be dehumanizing and blaming. The effects of all of this can devastate self-esteem and get in the way of healing and physical and emotional wellness. Your work is counteracting these devastating scenarios.

Working with Individuals

Many people like to have someone support them as they work on developing their WRAPs. If you are that support person, you can use the following steps as a guide in doing this work.

- If possible, have the person read through this book before you begin so they have a basic understanding of the task you are about to undertake and so they will be clear about the benefits of following the plan.

- Review the Wellness Toolbox Checklist in the appendix. Ask if there are any tools they have questions about. If they have questions, review the pertinent section and/or seek out other resources that might help. Then have them check off those tools that they feel would work for them and cross off those that they would never consider using.

- Help them discover other tools they have used successfully. To discover these tools, ask them to describe a time when they were not feeling well. Then ask them to identify those things they did to help themselves feel better. If they are not among those suggested in this book, add them.

There are two ways you could go from here. Both of them will be described. The person who is developing the WRAP should decide which approach they want to use.

Approach A

You could start with the crisis planning section and work back through the process. This is often the easiest way because the things that have the worst pain attached to them are the things that are remembered most vividly. Working with someone to remember, think about, and pay attention to the things that led up to the crisis is very helpful. It's easy to remember being flat on your back in pain for days. It's easy to forget that you didn't tell your friend on that long car trip that you needed to stop and walk for ten minutes each hour, or that you didn't call and talk to a friend after your thirteen-year-old told you that you were the worst parent in the world, or that your community commitments didn't allow you to get the rest breaks that you needed.

Using this strategy, at each phase you think about what would have helped move you back to the preceding section. You can use a series of questions to help someone with this process, such as:

- What was going on in your life just before you started feeling this bad or before the situation got this bad?

- What could you have done at that point that would have kept the situation from worsening?

- What could you do to keep things from getting this bad again?

- What signs did you ignore that could have told you that things needed to be done differently?

The advantage of this approach is that the plan is developed by analyzing a previous crisis and looking at how it could have been avoided. Following are a few examples for this approach.

Sally

Sally was experiencing severe disabling pain so that others needed to take over for her (a crisis situation). What could have happened to move her back to the place where she could take care of herself? The ideas she thought of were as follows: When the pain was getting intense and she was having a hard time walking and getting comfortable, which she labeled as when things were breaking down, she could have taken warm baths, used warm packs, had bed rest, increased the use of a magnesium malate (a food supplement) prescribed by her physician to be taken as needed, called her doctor and arranged an appointment, done several relaxation exercises a day, asked family members to take over her household responsibilities, gotten a gentle massage, and watched some funny videos.

Were there some early warning signs that she could have responded to that would have kept her from getting so much worse? Now she remembered that before her symptoms got severe, she had noticed aching in her arms and legs. Warm baths and cutting back on her strenuous activity would have been good responses at that point. A talk with her spouse would also have been a good idea.

Looking back even further, she discovered that there were some triggers that had probably begun the recurrence of this intensive pain cycle. A four-hour ride in a car with only one short break, along with raking the yard for two hours, were significant triggers. In addition, she was feeling really tense as a result of a disagreement with one of her children. She could have responded to these triggers by stopping for a ten-minute break every hour during the car trip (that would have meant leaving forty minutes earlier, but it would have been well worth it), reducing the amount of time spent raking the lawn to thirty minutes or asking someone else to do it for her, and spending some time talking to a good friend about the difficulties she'd been having with her child and doing a relaxation exercise.

In looking back at this scenario, she pinpointed things she needed to do every day to keep herself well—her daily maintenance plan. They included:

- thirty minutes of moderate outdoor exercise

- fifteen minutes of the stretching exercises prescribed by her physical therapist

- a daily fifteen minute relaxation exercise

- a warm bath every day

- checking in with a close supporter every day

- drinking at least eight, eight-ounce glasses of water daily

- eating three healthy meals

- avoiding long periods of time in a stationary position or doing physical labor

Approach B

The other way you can work with people developing their WRAPs is to design the daily maintenance plan, then determine the triggers and develop a response plan, then move on to early warning signs and the corresponding response plan. After this, focus on the stage when things are breaking down, again creating a response plan, and then, finally, develop a crisis plan. The advantage of this approach is that you begin with the daily maintenance plan, which many people feel is the easiest part of the plan, and then go on to progressively harder parts—triggers, early warning signs, and when things are breaking down—finishing with the crisis plan, which is hardest for most people.

For example, Jack is an older man with a chronic heart condition. He is much more familiar with what he needs to do every day to keep himself well and has not experienced a heart attack, which would be a severe crisis. When developing his WRAP, he began with the daily maintenance plan, listing the things he needed to do for himself every day. It included:

- strict adherence to his cholesterol and weight reduction diet

- forty-five minutes of moderate walking or other aerobic exercise

- taking prescribed food supplements and medications

- doing two twenty-minute meditation exercises (one in the morning and one in the evening)

- working in his wood shop for at least one hour

Jack identified the following triggers that might cause an increase in chest pain, weight, and cholesterol levels:

- eating in a fast-food restaurant where the desserts are on display

- getting in an argument with a friend or family member

- feeling pressured at work

- having car trouble

His plan for responding to these possible triggers if they occurred included:

- carrying fresh fruit to eat after the meal instead of having a rich dessert

- having a supply of fat free frozen yogurt on hand at home for dessert

- doing at least one extra meditation exercise

- spending an hour relaxing listening to a favorite opera

- talking to a supporter about problems, working out a solution, and taking positive action

Jack's early warning signs included:

- feeling nervous and anxious

- mild sweating

- getting out of breath slightly more easily than usual
- feeling unusually tired

    If these occurred he would:

- call his doctor, describe his symptoms, and follow the doctor's instructions
- ask someone else to take over all of his responsibilities for the day, including asking someone to drive him to the doctor if needed
- ask someone to stay with him for the rest of the day
- lean back in his lounge chair and listen to good music

    Jack would know that things were getting much worse—that things were breaking down—if he:

- began to experience pain in his chest and arms
- sweated more than usual
- had a hard time breathing
- felt nauseous

    His action plan for this time would be to:

- immediately call emergency services for transportation to the hospital
- alert anyone close by
- sit and listen to calming music while waiting for transportation

    Jack's definition of a crisis would be a heart attack. His crisis plan describes for his supporters what symptoms would indicate he was having a heart attack. They would include:

- being in severe pain
- having a pale complexion
- sweating
- being unconscious or semiconscious

Jack's crisis plan instructs his supporters on how to do CPR (they have all had CPR training as well). His plan specifies who is to be called and how he is to be transported to the hospital. It also describes household responsibilities that need to be taken care of, like feeding the cat and turning down the heat.

Working with Groups on Developing WRAPs

Developing WRAPs is well-suited to group work. I have worked with many groups, both large and small, in developing these plans. I begin by introducing participants to the WRAP process by going over each step. Then I describe some of the most common tools or responses. You can add any that you don't find in this book but feel would be helpful. As I describe each of these topics, I write it on a large sheet of paper. Then I ask the participants to share responses that have worked for them and write them on the paper. I keep this list posted for reference as WRAPs are developed. Following is a sample of such a list:

- getting support
- focusing
- fun activities
- light exposure
- (Other ideas from the group)

- peer counseling
- relaxation exercises
- diet changes
- daily planning

_____

_____

_____

_____

I then post five blank sheets of paper with the five headings (daily maintenance plan, triggers, early warning signs, when things are breaking down, and crisis) posted next to each other on a wall in the room. I add an additional blank sheet at the bottom of each sheet for action plans or responses. Because there are many sections of the crisis plan, the logistics of this arrangement may be difficult. For this section, you may choose to have sheets for only the "symptoms" and "help from others" sections.

If it is a large group or there is a limited amount of time, I describe each section of the plan and ask for audience input on both symptoms and responses, recording participant responses on newsprint sheets to give both an auditory and visual cue. This gives them an opportunity to take notes on any they feel are relevant to their situation. If there is space available, hang five sheets of newsprint across the front of the room, one for each section of the plan—beginning with the daily maintenance plan. Add additional sheets below the top sheet for each page of that section of the plan.

You can begin with the daily maintenance plan and work through the plan from there, or you can work from the crisis planning, moving back through the plan to the daily maintenance plan. The previous section in this chapter describes the benefits and procedures of both approaches.

If you are working with a smaller group and you have plenty of time, the following presentation plan is very effective. Begin by describing the different parts of the WRAP and developing a list of wellness tools (see the appendix for the Wellness Toolbox list, which can serve as a great starting place for your group's list). Ask a person in the group to volunteer to share their most troublesome symptoms. I put these on a newsprint sheet. For instance, Frank shared the following list: anger, crying, not eating, irritability, destroying things that are important to me, and hanging out in bars.

Take these symptoms, one at a time, and, getting feedback from the group, break them down. For example, anger means different things to different people. To find out what it means to Frank, I ask questions for more information. They include:

- Can you describe your anger?

- What's it like?

- What do you do when you are angry?

- How would other people describe your anger?

- What do you do when your anger is really bad?

Frank responds, "I get really argumentative. If someone says the sky is blue, I'll disagree. I get very livid. It really scares people."

Then I ask, "What's it like before this? Is there anything you were thinking or feeling? What was going on in your life?"

His response is: "I was thinking that people are against me and don't believe me. Also, I just realized that, before that, I was not getting enough attention from other people. I was spending too much time alone."

Give the person time to think when you are going through this process. Go slow. As you talk about the symptoms, the process becomes clear. In this circumstance, Frank realized that he had been *triggered* by events that he interpreted as rejecting or abandoning. His *early warning signs* were spending too much time alone and not connecting with his support people, as well as thinking that people didn't care about him and didn't like him. I wrote these on the appropriate sheets. *When things are breaking down* for Frank, he avoids people and thinks people are out to get him. A *crisis* for Frank is "when people seek me out and I argue with them and yell and scream at them."

Frank realized through this questioning process that, in his daily maintenance plan, he needed to include being in contact with at least one support person and being involved in one activity with others.

Frank then went on to work on another symptom: crying. It was easier for him this time because he was beginning to understand the process. He said, "When it's really bad, I'm usually alone. I can cry for hours—even all day. I obsess about all the bad things that have ever happened to me—how alone I am—and I think that I will never have anyone special in my life. That's when I start destroying things that are important to me. Then I head for the bars."

While Frank talked, I put his responses down on the different sheets according to where they fit in the plan. A picture began to emerge. This should be a logical process from beginning to end. If it becomes illogical, ask questions until it sorts itself out.

The sheets looked like this:

Daily Maintenance Plan	• be in contact with at least one support person
	• be involved in one activity with others

Triggers	• events that are interpreted as rejecting or abandoning
	• a friend failing to call up
	• a person ignoring him
Early Warning Signs	• spending too much time alone
	• not connecting with support people
	• thinking people don't care about him
	• thinking people don't like him
When Things Are Breaking Down	• avoiding people
	• avoiding friends
	• thinking people are out to get him
Crisis	• arguing
	• yelling and screaming at people
	• destroying property
	• hanging out in bars

Continue to ask questions and get more information that can be used in the WRAP, helping the person discover those feelings, symptoms, or actions that preceded difficult times. Asked a question like, "What was happening before you started destroying your things?" Frank replied, "I was telling myself repeatedly that I wasn't worth anything."

Once this part of the process is done and the symptoms are clarified, you begin the planning part of the process. If the steps for the symptoms are clear, the plan begins to become obvious. Where, when, and how to implement the tools is the next step. I use input from the whole group to do this. Use the sheets you have hung underneath the top sheet to develop the response plans.

Using this system, the person developing the plan figures out when, where, why, and how to use these skills/tools. This facilitates the use of the WRAP. It works much better than when someone tells someone else to do something because it's "good for them."

I have found that the brainstorming activity (chapter 5) is an excellent tool for working with groups. It helps groups work together to find solutions for individual problems.

Jane Winterling says:

As a teacher, I have been given the knowledge about the process and the courage it takes to heal from the real experts—the people who have to deal with these symptoms and issues every day. If there is any gift you can give yourself, I hope it is to let others teach you as well. It's our job as helpers to assist people in making some sense out of symptoms and situations that often seem to make no sense—and being able to do so is a gift for ourselves as well as those we help. I hope this work brings you as much joy as it has brought me.

Appendix

Duplicate Forms for Your WRAP

Chapter 1

Your Goals

"I want to use my WRAP to address the following issues":

_____

_____

_____

_____

Chapter 2

Your Reminder of Wellness

"When I feel well, I am":

_____

_____

_____

_____

_____

Your Daily Maintenance Plan

Things you must do every day:

_____

_____

_____

_____

_____

_____

Your Daily Reminder List

"Today I might need to":

_____

_____

_____

_____

_____

_____

Your Daily Optional Reminder List

Things that need to be done less frequently than daily but more than weekly:

_____

_____

_____

_____

Your Weekly Reminder List

Activity   **Day of the week**

_____

_____

_____

_____

Your Biweekly Reminder List

Activity   **When**

_____

_____

_____

_____

Your Monthly Reminder List

Activity   **When**

_____

_____

_____

_____

Chapter 3

Your List of Triggers

_____

_____

_____

_____

_____

_____

Things to Avoid to Prevent Being Triggered

_____

_____

_____

_____

_____

Your Plan for Responding to Triggers

_____

_____

_____

_____

_____

_____

_____

Early Warning Signs

Your Early Warning Signs:

_____

_____

_____

_____

_____

_____

Things you must do when you recognize early warning signs:

_____

_____

_____

_____

_____

_____

Things you may choose to do when you recognize early warning signs:

_____

_____

_____

_____

_____

_____

When Things Are Breaking Down

Signs of potential crisis:

_____

_____

_____

_____

_____

_____

Required responses to these signs:

_____

_____

_____

_____

_____

_____

Optional responses to these signs:

_____

_____

_____

_____

_____

_____

Updating Your Response Plan to Signs of Potential Crisis

Are there some symptoms or signs that should be added to your list? y _____
n _____ If so, what are they:

_____

_____

_____

_____

_____

Are there symptoms or signs that should be removed from your list? y _____
n _____ If so, what are they:

_____

_____

_____

_____

_____

Did your response plan work? y _____ n _____ If not, how could it be
changed so that it would be more effective next time?

_____

_____

_____

_____

_____

Chapter 4

Crisis Plan

Part 1: What I'm Like When I'm Feeling Well

Include all of the qualities you checked off, as well as any additional traits you listed.

_____

_____

_____

_____

_____

Part 2: Crisis Signs and Symptoms

Include all of the qualities you checked off, as well as any additional traits you listed.

_____

_____

_____

_____

Part 3: Supporters

List the attributes you would like from your supporters (both from the check list and your additional list):

_____

_____

_____

_____

You may want to name some people for certain tasks, like taking care of the children or paying the bills, and others for tasks like staying with you and taking you to health care appointments.

Name   **Connection/Role**   **Phone number**   **Specific Tasks**

_____

_____

_____

_____

_____

_____

Also list your health care professionals, their phone numbers, and their role in your treatment and care; this will allow your supporters to contact them when necessary.

Physician _____ Phone Number _____

When to contact _____

Pharmacist _____ Phone Number _____

When to contact _____

Other health care professionals

Name _____ Phone Number _____

Specialty _____

When to contact _____

Name _____ Phone Number _____

Specialty _____

When to contact _____

Name _____ Phone Number _____

Specialty _____

When to contact _____

Name _____ Phone Number _____

Specialty _____

When to contact _____

I *do not* want the following people involved in any way in my care or treatment:

Name   **Why you do not want them involved (optional)**

_____

_____

_____

_____

I want disputes between my supporters settled as follows:

_____

_____

_____

_____

Part 4: Medication

Questions to Ask the Doctor About Medication

generic name _____ product name _____

product category _____

suggested dosage level _____

How does this medication work? What do you expect it to do?

_____

_____

How long will it take to achieve that result?

_____

What are the risks associated with taking this medication?

_____

_____

What kind of an effectiveness track record does this medication have?

_____

What short-term side effects does this medication have?

_____

_____

_____

What long-term side effects does this medication have?

_____

_____

_____

Is there any way to minimize the chances of experiencing these side effects? If so, what are they?

_____

_____

_____

Are there any dietary or lifestyle suggestions or restrictions when using this medication?

_____

_____

_____

_____

Why do you recommend this particular medication?

_____

_____

_____

_____

Have you had other patients who have used it? _____ If so, how have they done?

_____

_____

_____

How is this medication monitored?

_____

_____

_____

What tests will I need prior to taking this medication?

_____

_____

How often will I need these tests while taking the medication?

_____

_____

What symptoms indicate that the dosage should be changed or the medication stopped?

_____

_____

_____

Your physician, in working with your supporters, may recommend a medication that you have not studied. Name a supporter or several supporters who could fill out this form for you, so that they have needed information to decide if the medication should be used.

Supporter to study recommended medications _____

List any allergies you have that would affect medication decisions:

_____

_____

_____

List the medications you are currently using, the dosage, why you are taking them, and other pertinent information.

Medication	Dosage	Purpose	Other Information

List those medications you would prefer to take if medications or additional medications became necessary, and explain why you would choose to use them.

Medication	Why I Prefer to Use This Medication

List those medications that would be acceptable to you if medications became necessary, and why you would choose them.

Medication	Why I Would Find This Medication Acceptable

List those medications that you don't want to use and give the reasons why.

Medication	Why I Don't Want to Use It

Part 5: Treatments

Treatments you'd be willing to try in the event of a crisis:

_____

_____

_____

_____

_____

Treatments you *wouldn't* be willing to try in the event of a crisis:

_____

_____

_____

_____

_____

Part 6: Options for Short-term and Long-term Care

If I need home care, the following person/people have agreed to act as care-team leaders:

_____

_____

_____

_____

_____

The following people have agreed to help provide me with home care in the event of a crisis.

Name   **Phone Number**   **Availability Information (e.g., nights only)**

_____

_____

_____

_____

Home care services to contact if necessary   Phone   Services

Doctor(s) who may be willing to make a house call   Phone

**Rescue personnel to be advised in case
my condition becomes life threatening**   Phone

**Community care and/or
respite programs**   Phone   When to be used

Part 7: Hospital Care

Attributes that are important to you in choosing a hospital facility:

If I need hospitalization or treatment in a treatment facility, I prefer the following facilities in order of preference:

Name	Contact	Person	Phone Number

I prefer this facility because:

Name	Contact	Person	Phone Number

I prefer this facility because:

Name	Contact	Person	Phone Number

I prefer this facility because:

Name	Contact	Person	Phone Number

I prefer this facility because:

Avoid using the following hospital or treatment facilities:

Name	Reason to avoid using

Part 8: Help from Others

Describe in as much detail as possible:

- what you anticipate needing from others in the event of a crisis
- interventions that have helped in the past
- interventions that you think might help
- specific tasks for specific people
- interventions or actions that should be avoided

Things you need your supporters to do for you to help reduce symptoms and keep you safe (from the check list and your additional list):

_____

_____

_____

_____

**Things you need others to do
for you**   **Who you want to do it**
_____

_____

_____

_____

_____

_____

Things that would not help or might even worsen your symptoms:

_____

_____

_____

_____

Part 9: When Your Supporters No Longer Need to Use This Plan

Your supporters no longer need to take care of you when:

_____

_____

_____

_____

Chapter 5

Wellness Toolbox Checklist

Use this list as a reminder of the tools described in chapters 5–8. Check off the ones that you felt would work for you. Add to the list any other responses you have thought of. Then use this list in maintaining and updating your WRAP.

Lifestyle Issues

❑ Educate yourself

❑ Exercise

❑ Diet

❑ Light

❑ Daily planning

❑ Brainstorming

❑ Do something normal

Health-Related Responses

❑ Get a physical examination

❑ Get a medication check

❑ Talk to a health care professional about a change in your treatment regime

❑ Get a second opinion

❑ Get a referral to a specialist

❑ Use hot or cold packs

❑ Get supportive therapies

❑ Get a massage

❑ Give yourself a massage

❑ Acupuncture

❑ Acupressure

❑ Vitamin, mineral, herbal, homeopathic, or other food supplementation

Developing a Strong Support System

❑ Peer counseling

❑ Ask someone else to help you out

❑ Counseling

- ❏ Call a warm line
- ❏ Call a hot line
- ❏ Host a potluck supper or some other meal
- ❏ Have a meeting of your supporters or your family

Changing the Way You Feel about Yourself

- ❏ Surround yourself with people who are positive, affirming, and loving
- ❏ Wear something that makes you feel good
- ❏ Look through old pictures, scrapbooks, and photo albums
- ❏ Make a collage of your life
- ❏ Make a list of your accomplishments
- ❏ Spend ten minutes writing down everything good you can think of about yourself
- ❏ Do something that makes you laugh
- ❏ Do something special for someone else
- ❏ Pretend you are your own best friend
- ❏ Get some little things done
- ❏ Repeat positive affirmations

Relieving Tension and Stress

- ❏ Yoga
- ❏ Be present in the moment
- ❏ Take a warm bath
- ❏ Look at something pretty or that means something special to you
- ❏ Play with children or a pet
- ❏ Do focusing exercises
- ❏ Do breathing awareness exercises
- ❏ Deep breathing
- ❏ Progressive relaxation
- ❏ Guided imagery
- ❏ Auralizing

Affecting the Senses

❏ Exposing yourself to something that smells good to you

❏ Responding visually

❏ Getting a massage

❏ Listening to music

❏ Making music

❏ Singing

Other Responses You Have Discovered:

_____

_____

_____

_____

Daily Planning Form

7:00–8:00 A.M.

_____

_____

8:00–9:00 A.M.

_____

_____

9:00–10:00 A.M.

_____

_____

10:00–11:00 A.M.

_____

_____

11:00–12:00 NOON

_____

_____

12:00–1:00 P.M.

_____

_____

1:00–2:00 P.M.

_____

_____

2:00–3:00 PM..

_____

_____

3:00–4:00 PM..

_____

_____

4:00–5:00 P.M.

_____

_____

5:00–6:00 P.M.

_____

_____

6:00–7:00 P.M.

_____

_____

7:00–8:00 P.M.

_____

_____

8:00–9:00 P.M.

_____

_____

9:00–10:00 P.M.

_____

_____

10:00 P.M.

_____

_____

Brainstorming

Situation or circumstance that needs to be addressed

_____

_____

_____

_____

Will you do the brainstorming exercise alone y _____ n _____ . If no, who will you do the exercise with?

_____ , _____ , _____ , _____

_____ , _____ , _____ , _____

Ideas and suggestions

_____

_____

_____

_____

_____

Of the ideas, which are actions that would be helpful to take right away?

_____

_____

_____

_____

Which are actions that you can include in your WRAP?

_____

_____

_____

_____

_____

Which are actions that are not feasible to take at this time?

_____

_____

_____

_____

_____

Creative or Diversionary Activities

Creative or diversionary activities that you want to include in your WRAP:

_____

_____

_____

_____

_____

Chapter 6

Information for the Physician

1. All medications, vitamins, and health care preparations you are using for any reason.

Medication	Dosage	When	How Used

2. A medical history of yourself and your family.

Your history

Your Mother's Side of the Family

Your Father's Side of the Family

3. Describe changes in the following aspects of your health.

Your appetite or diet: _____

_____

Your weight: _____

_____

Your sleep patterns: _____

_____

Your sexual interest: _____

_____

Your ability to concentrate: _____

_____

Your memory: _____

_____

Have you recently had:

❏ headaches (describe) _____

❏ numbness or tingling anywhere (where) _____

❏ loss of balance (describe) _____

❏ double vision or vision problems (describe) _____

❏ periods of amnesia (describe) _____

❏ coordination changes (describe) _____

❏ weakness in arms or legs (describe) _____

❏ fever (describe) _____

❏ nausea or diarrhea (describe) _____

❏ other gastrointestinal problems (describe) _____

❏ fainting or dizziness (describe) _____

❏ seizures (describe) _____

❏ stressful life events (describe) _____ _____

Add additional sheets for other pertinent information.

Support List

Name	Phone Number	Activities to Share

Chapter 7

Negative Thoughts and/or Attitudes that
Cause You Worry or Discomfort

_____

_____

_____

_____

_____

Checking the Validity of Negative Thoughts

Your negative thought:

_____

_____

Ask yourself the following questions about the thought. Be honest with yourself. Skip over those questions that do not apply to your negative thoughts or attitudes.

1. Is this negative thought or attitude really true? (Give yourself the benefit of the doubt. Provide supporting evidence to the contrary.)
   [Sample answer in response to "I never do anything right": It's not really true. I do lots of things very well. They include: cooking, gardening, driving a car, and caring for my child.]

_____

_____

_____

_____

2. Would a person who really cares about you be thinking this about you? If not, then should you be saying it to yourself?
   [Sample response to "I never do anything right": No one who really cared about a person would ever think, "They can't do anything right." So I shouldn't be saying it to myself.]

_____

_____

_____

_____

_____

3. Ask other people you trust: Do you think this negative thought or attitude is true?
   [Sample response to "I never do anything right": My friend said of course that wasn't true. She pointed out how successful I am at work and reminded me that she thought I was a good friend, and that being her friend was something that I had done really well.]

_____

_____

_____

_____

4. What do you get out of thinking your negative thought or attitude? How does it help? How does it hurt?
   [Sample response to "I never do anything right": I don't get anything out of saying to myself "I can't do anything right." It makes me feel terrible. It causes me to worry about things.]

_____

_____

_____

_____

Developing Positive Thoughts to Contradict Negative Ones

[Sample response to "I never do anything right": I could say, "I do lots of things right."]

Write a positive statement that is the opposite of your negative thought.

_____

_____

Make a list of positive affirmations that would help you feel better (including any from the list of examples that you think you'd benefit from):

Repeating Affirmations

_____

_____

_____

_____

_____

_____

Chapter 8

List all of the relaxation and stress reduction exercises that you wish to use from chapter 8:

_____

_____

_____

_____

Chapter 9

Adapting Your WRAP

Advance Planning Worksheet

Describe anticipated event or circumstance

_____

_____

When will it occur, or when is it likely to occur?

_____

_____

What actions could you take in advance to ease the situation and when could you take them?

_____

_____

_____

_____

(Focus on one action at a time for the following questions. Use photocopies of this form to address each action possible.) Who will you need to ask for help to get this done?

_____

_____

_____

_____

How will you implement this action?

_____

_____

_____

_____

How will taking this action help?

_____

_____

_____

_____

What purchases need to be made?

_____

_____

_____

_____

If you don't have the money readily available to make these purchases, how could you make this happen (credit cards, loan from a bank or family member, savings, grants from local or government organizations, etc.)?

_____

_____

_____

_____

Put the copies in your WRAP binder.

For Situations without Advance Warning

In case of a sudden loss or disaster with no warning, I think the following would be helpful to me:

_____

_____

_____

_____

Resources

Publications, Phone Numbers, and Software Programs That Can Help You in Developing Your WRAP

Addictions

Birkedahl, N. 1990. *The Habit Control Workbook.* Oakland, Calif.: New Harbinger Publications, Inc.

Catalano, E., and N. Sonenberg. 1993. *Consuming Passions: Help for Compulsive Shoppers.* Oakland, Calif.: New Harbinger Publications, Inc.

Center for Substance Abuse Prevention (SAMSHA). 1997. *National Clearinghouse for Alcohol and Drug Information Publications Catalog.* Washington, D.C.: Center for Substance Abuse, Substance Abuse and Mental Health Services Administration (SAMSHA).

Fanning, P., and J. O'Neill. 1996. *The Addiction Workbook: A Step-by-Step Guide to Quitting Alcohol & Drugs.* Oakland, Calif.: New Harbinger Publications, Inc.

Tanner, L. 1996. *The Mother's Survival Guide to Recovery: All about Alcohol, Drugs, and Babies.* Oakland, Calif.: New Harbinger Publications, Inc.

Roselline, G., and M. Worden. 1997. *Of Course You're Angry: A Guide to Dealing with the Emotions of Substance Abuse.* Center City, Minn.: Hazeldon.

Roth, G. 1993. *Breaking Free from Compulsive Eating.* New York: NAL-Dutton.

Stevic-Rust, L., and A. Maxmin. 1996. *The Stop Smoking Workbook: Your Guide to Healthy Quitting.* Oakland, Calif.: New Harbinger Publications, Inc.

AIDS

The CDC National AIDS Information and Referral Hotline twenty-four-hour line: 800-342-AIDS
The National AIDS Clearinghouse educational resources: 800-458-5231
The People with AIDS Coalition: 800-828-3280
Project Inform treatment and therapies: 800-822-7422

Cancer

Gersh, W., W. Golden, and D. Robbins. 1997. *Mind over Malignancy: Living with Cancer.* Oakland, Calif.: New Harbinger Publications, Inc.

Love, S. with K. Lindsay. 1995. *Dr. Susan Love's Breast Book.* New York: Addison-Wesley Publishing Co.

Career and Work Issues

Bolles, R. 1996. *What Color Is Your Parachute?* 1997. Berkeley, Calif.: Ten Speed Press.

Hakim, C. 1994. *We Are All Self-Employed: The New Social Contract for Working in a Changed World.* San Francisco, Calif.: Berrett-Koehler Publishers.

O'Hara, V. 1995. *Wellness at Work: Building Resilience to Job Stress.* Oakland, Calif.: New Harbinger Publications, Inc.

Caretaking

Levin, N. 1997. *How to Care for Your Parents: A Practical Guide to Eldercare.* New York: W. W. Norton & Co.

Changing Negative Thoughts to Positive Ones

Burns, D. 1990. *The Feeling Good Handbook.* New York: Plume.

Cash, T. 1997. *The Body Image Workbook: An Eight-Step Program for Learning to Like Your Looks.* Oakland, Calif.: New Harbinger Publications, Inc.

Fanning, P., and M. McKay. 1991. *Prisoners of Belief.* Oakland, Calif.: New Harbinger Publications.

Copeland, M. E. 1992. *The Depression Workbook: A Guide to Living with Depression and Manic Depression.* Oakland, Calif.: New Harbinger Publications.

McKay, M., M. Davis, and P. Fanning. 1997. *Thoughts and Feelings.* Oakland, Calif.: New Harbinger Publications.

Depression

Copeland, M. E. 1995. *Coping with Depression* audio tape. Oakland, Calif.: New Harbinger Publications, Inc.

———. 1994. *Living with Depression* video tape. Oakland, Calif.: New Harbinger Publications, Inc.

———. 1994. *Living Without Depression and Manic Depression: A Workbook for Maintaining Mood Stability.* Oakland, Calif.: New Harbinger Publications, Inc.

————. 1992. *The Depression Workbook: A Guide for Living with Depression and Manic Depression.* Oakland, Calif.: New Harbinger Publications, Inc.

Real, T. 1997. *I Don't Want to Talk about It: Overcoming the Secret Legacy of Male Depression.* New York: Simon & Schuster.

Emotional and Mental Health Issues

Bourne, E. 1995. *The Anxiety and Phobia Workbook,* 2nd ed. Oakland, Calif.: New Harbinger Publications, Inc.

Finney, L. 1996. *Clear Your Past, Change Your Future: Proven Techniques for Inner Exploration and Healing.* Oakland, Calif.: New Harbinger Publications, Inc.

Markway, B., C. Carmin, C. Pollard, and T. Flynn. 1992. *Dying Of Embarrassment: Help for Social Anxiety and Social Phobia.* Oakland, Calif.: New Harbinger Publications, Inc.

McKay, M., and P. Fanning. 1993. *Self-Esteem,* 2nd ed. Oakland, Calif.: New Harbinger Publications, Inc.

Steketee, G., and K. White. 1990. *When Once Is Not Enough: Help for Obsessive Compulsives.* Oakland, Calif.: New Harbinger Publications, Inc.

White, B., and E. Madera, eds. 1997. *The Self-Help Source Book: Finding and Forming Mutual Aid Self-Help Groups.* Denville, N.J.: American Self-Help Clearinghouse, Northwest Covenant Medical Center. To order, call 201-625-7101.

Wolpe, J. 1988. *Life Without Fear: Anxiety and Its Cure.* Oakland, Calif.: New Harbinger Publications, Inc.

Zuercher-White, E. 1995. *An End to Panic: Breakthrough Techniques for Overcoming Panic Disorder.* Oakland, Calif.: New Harbinger Publications, Inc.

Exercise Programs

Schatz, M., and W. Conner. 1992. *Back Care Basics: A Doctor's Gentle Yoga Program for Back and Neck Pain Relief.* Berkeley, Calif.: Rodmell Press.

Tobias, M., and J. Sullivan. 1992. *Complete Stretching: A New Exercise Program for Health and Vitality.* New York: Alfred A. Knopf, Inc.

Nelson, M. 1998. *Strong Women Stay Young.* New York: Bantam Trade Paperback.

Financial Concerns

Dominguez, J., and V. Robin. 1992. *Your Money or Your Life: Transforming Your Relationship with Money and Achieving Financial Independence.* New York: Penguin Books.

Hunt, M. 1997. *The Complete Cheapskate: How to Break Free from the Money Worries Forever, Without Sacrificing the Quality of Your Life.* Colorado Springs, Colo.: Focus on the Family Publishers.

————. 1995. *The Cheapskate Monthly Money Makeover.* New York: St. Martin's Press.

Loungo, T. 1997. *Ten Minute Guide to Household Budgeting.* Indianapolis, Ind.: Macmillan General Reference.

McCullough, B. 1996. *Bonnie's Household Budget Book: The Essential Workbook for Getting Control of Your Money.* New York: St. Martin's Press.

Software

Quicken Deluxe 98; Quicken Home and Business 98; Money 98; The Stock Shop with Peter Lynch; Window on Wall Street: Deluxe Investor; Managing Your Money 2.0; Versa Check. Comp USA Direct: 800-899-6204.

Focusing

Cornell, A. 1996. *The Power of Focusing.* Oakland, Calif.: New Harbinger Publications.

Gendlin, E. 1981. *Focusing.* New York: Bantam Books.

Getting Organized

Covey, S. 1996. *First Things First.* New York: Fireside Books.

Software

Day-Timer Organizer 98; Lotus Organizer 97 GS; Ecco Pro, ACT!; Project Manager Pro; Small Business Start-Up; Success Inc: Business Plan Business; Plan Pro. Comp USA Direct: 800-899-6204.

Health Information

Benson, H., and E. Stuart. 1992. *The Wellness Book: The Comprehensive Guide to Maintaining Health and Treating Stress-Related Illness.* New York: Simon & Schuster.

Boston Women's Health Collective. 1992. *The New Our Bodies, Ourselves.* New York: Simon & Schuster.

Catalano, E., and K. Hardin. 1996. *The Chronic Pain Control Workbook.* Oakland, Calif.: New Harbinger Publications, Inc.

Crook, W. 1986. *The Yeast Connection: A Medical Breakthrough.* New York: Vintage.

Doress-Worters, P., and D. Siegal, in cooperation with the Boston Women's Health Collective. 1996. *The New Ourselves Growing Older: Women Aging With Knowledge and Power.* New York: Peter Smith Press.

Goldberg, B. 1993. *Alternative Medicine Guide to Chronic Fatigue, Fibromyalgia, and Environmental Illness.* Tiburon, Calif.: Future Medicine Publishers.

Langer, S. 1995. *Solved: The Riddle of Illness.* New Canaan, Conn.: Keats Publishing.

Ostrom, N. 1993. *Fifty Things You Should Know about Chronic Fatigue Syndrome.* New York: St. Martin's Press.

Sears, B., and W. Lawren. 1995. *The Zone: A Dietary Road Map.* New York: Harper-Collins Publishers.

Starlanyl, D., and M. Copeland. 1996. *Fibromyalgia and Chronic Myofascial Pain Syndrome: A Survival Manual.* Oakland, Calif.: New Harbinger Publications.

Insomnia

Albert, K. 1996. *Get a Good Night's Sleep.* New York: Fireside Books.

Buchman, D. 1997. *The Complete Guide to Natural Sleep.* New Canaan, Conn.: Keats.

Journaling

Cameron, J., and M. Bryan. 1995. *The Artist's Way: A Spiritual Path to Higher Creativity.* New York: Putnam Publishing Group.

Progoff, I. 1992. *At a Journal Workshop: Writing to Access the Power of the Unconscious and Evoke Creative Ability.* New York: Putnam Publishing Group.

Seasonal Affective Disorder/Light Therapy

Rosenthal, N. 1993. *Winter Blues.* New York: Guilford Press.

Loss of a Loved One

Becker, M. 1993. *Last Touch: Preparing for a Parent's Death.* Oakland, Calif.: New Harbinger Publications, Inc.

Caplan, S., and G. Lang. 1995. *Grief's Courageous Journey: A Workbook.* Oakland, Calif.: New Harbinger Publications, Inc.

Doka, K. 1996. *Living with Grief after Sudden Loss: Suicide, Homicide, Accident, Heart Attack, Stroke.* Bristol, Pa.: Taylor & Francis.

Staudacher, C. 1987. *Beyond Grief: A Guide for Recovering from the Death of a Loved One.* Oakland, Calif.: New Harbinger Publications, Inc.

Nadeau, J. 1997. *Families Making Sense of Death.* Thousand Oaks, Calif.: Sage Publications, Inc.

Staudacher, C. 1992. *Men and Grief.* Oakland, Calif.: New Harbinger Publications, Inc.

Loneliness

Parker, H., and D. Virtue. 1996. *If This Is Love, Why Am I So Lonely?* Minneapolis, Minn.: Fairview Press.

Natural Healing

Balch, J., and P. Balch 1997. *Prescription for Nutritional Healing.* New York: Avery Publishing Group.

Cummings, S., and D. Ullman. 1984. *Everybody's Guide to Homeopathic Medicines: Taking Care of Yourself and Your Family with Safe and Effective Remedies.* New York: G. P. Putnam's Sons.

Fleischman, G., and C. Stein. 1997. *Acupuncture: Everything You Ever Wanted To Know but Were Afraid to Ask.* Barrytown, N.Y.: Barrytown Ltd.

Kenyon, J. 1996. *Acupressure Techniques: A Self-Help Guide.* Rochester, Vt.: Healing Arts Press.

Rector-Page, L. 1996. *Healthy Healing: A Guide to Self Healing for Everyone.* Calif.: Healthy Healing Publications.

Shen, P. 1996. *Massage for Pain Relief.* New York: Random House.

Ullman, D. 1995. *The Consumer's Guide to Homeopathy: The Definitive Resource for Understanding Homeopathic Medicine and Making It Work for You.* New York: G. P. Putnam's Sons.

Worwood, V. 1991. *The Complete Book of Essential Oils & Aromatherapy.* Novato, Calif.: New World Library.

Shen, P. 1996. *Massage for Pain Relief.* New York: Random House.

Parenting

Frain, B., and E. Clegg. 1997. *Becoming a Wise Parent for Your Grown Child: How to Give Love and Support Without Meddling.* Oakland, Calif.: New Harbinger Publications, Inc.

Newman, M. 1994. *Stepfamily Realities: How to Overcome Difficulties and Have a Happy Family.* Oakland, Calif.: New Harbinger Publications, Inc.

Paleg, K. 1997. *The Ten Things Every Parent Needs to Know: A Guide for New Parents and Everyone Else Who Cares about Children.* Oakland, Calif.: New Harbinger Publications, Inc.

Pantley, E. 1996. *Kid Cooperation: How to Stop Yelling, Nagging, and Pleading and Get Kids to Cooperate.* Oakland, Calif.: New Harbinger Publications, Inc.

Peer Counseling

Copeland, M. E. 1994. *Living Without Depression and Manic Depression: A Workbook for Maintaining Mood Stability.* Oakland, Calif.: New Harbinger Publications, Inc.

———. 1992. *The Depression Workbook: A Guide for Living with Depression and Manic Depression.* Oakland, Calif.: New Harbinger Publications, Inc.

Relationship Issues

Beattie, M. 1989. *Beyond Codependency.* New York: Harper & Row.

Brinegar, J. 1992. *Breaking Free from Domestic Violence.* Minneapolis, Minn.: CompCare Publishers.

Enns, G., and J. Black. 1997. *It's Not Okay Anymore: Your Personal Guide to Ending Abuse, Taking Charge, and Loving Yourself.* Oakland, Calif.: New Harbinger Publications, Inc.

Evans, P. 1992. *The Verbally Abusive Relationship: How to Recognize It and How to Respond.* Holbrook, Mass.: Bob Adams, Inc.

McKay, M., M. Davis, and P. Fanning. 1995. *Messages: The Communication Skills Book,* 2nd ed. Oakland, Calif.: New Harbinger Publications, Inc.

Savage, E. 1997. *Don't Take It Personally!: The Art of Dealing with Rejection.* Oakland, Calif.: New Harbinger Publications, Inc.

Scott, G. 1990. *Resolving Conflict: With Others and Within Yourself.* Oakland, Calif.: New Harbinger Publications, Inc.

Relaxation and Stress Reduction

Benson, H., and W. Proctor. 1985. *Beyond the Relaxation Response.* New York: Berkeley Press.

Campbell, D. 1989. *The Roar of Silence: Healing Powers of Breath, Tone, and Music.* Wheaton, Ill.: Theosophical Publishing House.

Fanning, P. 1994. *Visualization For Change*, 2d nd. Oakland, Calif.: New Harbinger Publications, Inc.

McKay, M., M. Davis, and P. Fanning. 1997. *Relaxation and Stress Reduction Workbook*, 4th ed. Oakland, Calif.: New Harbinger Publications.

McKay, M., and P. Fanning 1997. *The Daily Relaxer*. Oakland, Calif.: New Harbinger Publications, Inc.

O'Hara, V. 1996. *Five Weeks to Healing Stress: The Wellness Option*. Oakland, Calif.: New Harbinger Publications, Inc.

Ramacharaka, Y. 1996. *Science of Breath*. Eliot, Maine: Taraporevala Sons & Co.

Sky, M. 1990. *Breathing, Expanding Your Power and Energy*. Santa Fe, N. Mex.: Bear & Company Publishing, 1990.

Retirement

Clark, J. 1992. *Full Life Fitness: A Complete Exercise Program for Mature Adults*. Champaign, Ill.: Human Kinetics Pubs.

Fetridge, G. 1994. *The Adventure of Retirement: It's About Much More Than Just Money*. Amherst, N.Y.: Prometheus Books.

Sexuality Issues

Johnson, B. 1997. *Coming Out Every Day: A Gay, Bisexual, and Questioning Man's Guide*. Oakland, Calif.: New Harbinger Publications, Inc.

Surgery

Deardorff, W., and J. Reeves. 1997. *Preparing for Surgery: A Mind-Body Approach to Enhance Healing and Recovery*. Oakland, Calif.: New Harbinger Publications, Inc.

Trauma

Adams, C., and J. Fay. 1989. *Free of the Shadows: Recovering from Sexual Violence*. Oakland, Calif.: New Harbinger Publications, Inc.

Herman, J. 1992. *Trauma and Recovery: The Aftermath of Violence, from Domestic Abuse to Political Terror*. New York: Basic Books.

Matsakis, A. 1998. *Trust after Trauma: A Guide to Relationships for Survivors and Those Who Love Them*. Oakland, Calif.: New Harbinger Publications, Inc.

MENTAL HEALTH RECOVERY
Curriculum
including

Wellness Recovery Action Planning

Facilitator
Training Manual

By Mary Ellen Copeland, PhD

The *Facilitator Training Manual* with CD-ROM is an invaluable resource for anyone who is committed to sharing mental health self-help recovery information.

This comprehensive curriculum package includes:
- **Section I, Curriculum**: specific instructions for teaching recovery and WRAP in different circumstances and settings.
- **Section II, Transparencies**: both thumbnail sketches and a CD-Rom of over 200 workshop presentation transparencies.
- **Section III, Activities, Handouts and Discussion Topics**: suggestions for each topic, following the sequence of the transparencies, and handouts that may be copied and distributed.
- **Section IV, Resources**: an extensive listing of mental health resources for the facilitator.

The curriculum was originally designed for participants in training seminars. It has been revised to provide guidance to a broader audience of people teaching recovery who adhere to the values and guidelines outlined in the curriculum.

Facilitator Manual: Mental Health Recovery including WRAP _____ copies at $129.00

Subtotal $ _____

Shipping/Handling: total # curriculum x $8.00 per item _____

Total amount due _____

Name _____

Address_____

City and State _____ Zip _____

Phone_____ e-mail _____

Make checks payable to Mary Ellen Copeland.

( ) Mastercard ( ) Visa Card # _____ Expires _____

Mail order to: Mary Ellen Copeland, PO Box 301, West Dummerston, VT 05357-0301

Phone 802-254-2092   FAX 802-257-7499

E-mail: books@mentalhealthrecovery.com   Web site: www.mentalhealthrecovery.com